ON YEATS : UPON A HOUSE

NCQ TITLES

Legal Fictions

Politics & Letters

On Yeats: Upon a House

Drama & Democracy

Locating Theology

Time Pieces

Critical Paranoia

On Joyce: 3 easy essays

On Eliot

Literary Conversions

Film texts

A Trip to Rome

A Short Break in Budapest

Magic in Prague

A Week in Venice

Four Days in Athens

The Last Priest of Horus

WWW: the weekend that warped the world

Play texts

Darwin: an evolutionary entertainment

Strange Meetings & Shorts

Eliotics

Forthcoming

Rubbishing Hockney & other reviews

On Collecting Walter Benjamin

Autobiography & Class Consciousness

Considering Canterbury Cathedral

Though each can be read independently,
these NCQ publications, taken together,
comprise a single hyper-text collection.

ON YEATS:

UPON A HOUSE

Bernard Sharratt

New Crisis Quarterly
2015

NEW CRISIS QUARTERLY

ncq@newcrisisquarterly.myzen.co.uk

First published 2015

ISBN : 978-1-910956-02-1

For
Grandma Armstrong
& all the Armstrongs,
O'Neills, and Conroys
who "came over"

UPON A HOUSE SHAKEN BY THE LAND AGITATION

How should the world be luckier if this house,
Where passion and precision have been one
Time out of mind, became too ruinous
To breed the lidless eye that loves the sun?
And the sweet laughing eagle thoughts that grow
Where wings have memory of wings, and all
That comes of the best knit to the best? Although
Mean roof-trees were the sturdier for its fall,
How should their luck run high enough to reach
The gifts that govern men, and after these
To gradual Time's last gift, a written speech
Wrought of high laughter, loveliness and ease?

FOREWORD

This short book offers an extended commentary expanding outwards from just one short poem by W. B. Yeats, exploring how we might make sense of its claims, the unfolding contexts in which we might read or locate it, and how we might now respond to it. Though unusually lengthy for an exercise in literary criticism based mainly upon a single poem, the book nevertheless remains incomplete, and in a sense unfinished, for reasons which will become clear. This very incompletedness is indeed part of what concerns me in the book.

Drafts of the book existed in three versions, all dating from the mid-1980s: as a lecture for the University of Liverpool; as a set of exercises for a day-long workshop for a sixth-form college in Chenin (Madras); and as the opening chapter of a book on the history of modern literature in Ireland, which was a reluctantly accepted and never completed commission from a publisher. All three versions have left traces in the conflated version offered here.

The imprint under which the book is now published, 'New Crisis Quarterly', revives the title of an exceedingly short-lived periodical: its first, only, and farewell issue appeared in 1984, under the guise of my *The Literary Labyrinth*. Its editorial programme was to publish reviews of books I didn't feel I had the time actually to write. So both the variously named reviewers and the variously authored reviewed books in *Literary Labyrinth* were therefore wholly imagined, but readers were invited, if so inclined, to write the books themselves.

So, as with other NCQ books, I offer this one partly in the spirit of that original editorial approach. Since it was *NCQ* policy to present texts which, in one way or another, leave work for the reader to undertake, the work-shop version of this exercise was particularly faithful to that emphasis: the various components of the 'commentary' were offered only in deliberately delayed stages during the workshop sessions, so that participants were gradually introduced to, and prompted to debate and assess, the significance of the partial unfolding of 'relevant historical facts' and their shifting impact upon their responses to the poem and to the issues raised. The printed form of the book is intended to encourage a similar delayed reaction, as the reader engages with the several issues intertwined in the commentary.

The text situates one such issue—how we might now arrive at an overall judgement on Yeats's own assessment of his work—by an indicative reading of 'Easter 1916', the poem rather than the event, and a consideration of how that poem can be situated within an overall account of a single volume published by Yeats in 1921, *Michael Robartes and the Dancer*. Here my own text begins to unravel, as other issues move to the forefront.

Insofar, for example, as 'Upon a House' itself raises the problem of the global import of literature and its political role, or irrelevance, aspects of the global transformations since its composition are sketchily considered, in part as the radically changed context in which the poem might 'now' be encountered, but also as exploring what seemed in the 1980s to be possible future developments in those global transformations. This component of the text was rather unsatisfactorily revised at a particular moment in the 1990s. Which raises again a concern apparent in the opening sections of the commentary: the complex and changing relations between reading, writing, the passing of time, and what we call history.

It will become clear, however, why this ever-expanding 'commentary' has finally been left un-concluded, indeed abandoned. Just as the poem itself responds to a specific moment in the long history of Ireland, this text too cannot escape from later moments in the complex history in which it sought to locate both the poem and itself. Whether readers will ever feel inclined to attempt a completion of this particular exercise may well depend upon further developments which the text itself cannot, of course, foresee.

The text is intended to be read consecutively and as an unfolding whole, but some section headings are indicated at the end of the essay for those who might want to re-read specific passages.

Finally, one over-arching invitation to readers remains: to complete, if they so wish, the partly failed and partly defeated attempts of my generation of literary critics to make the critical consideration of the relations between literature and politics a viable and effective contribution. Other preoccupations have rightly succeeded ours, but the underlying problems remain, and in the present context some of those previous emphases are worth, I still think, revisiting.

B.S.
May 10th
2015

reading in time

I sat most of this morning in my garden. A bright August day. Reading. An anthology of Irish verse. Including Sir Samuel Ferguson's clumsily un-recitable poem 'On the Death of Thomas Davis':

I walked through Ballinderry in the Spring-time,
When the bud was on the tree;
And I said, in every fresh-ploughed field beholding
The sowers striding free,
Scattering broad-cast forth the corn in golden plenty
On the quick seed-clasping soil,
Even such, this day, among the fresh-stirred hearts of Erin,
Thomas Davis, is thy toil!

And so on. Predictable. Dire. At stanza five, though, I paused.

And, alas! to think that now, and thou art lying,
Dear Davis, dead at thy mother's knee;
And I, no mother near, on my own sick-bed,
That face on earth shall never see . . .

It was the oddly appealing immediacy of the 'now', with its pausing comma, that finally struck me, together with the curious temporality, now, of that 'never', a never that was future for Ferguson: he would never again in the future see Thomas Davis. But for me a never in the past tense: I never did see either of them and never will. For me, historical figures. Texts from the past. An era almost unimaginably distant, it seems, now.

The poem was written, I found myself consciously registering, in 1845, at the height of the Great Famine in Ireland (despite that 'corn in golden plenty...'). Davis was recently dead at the age of thirty-one. Ferguson himself was then thirty-five. The poem mourns from a specific moment in history, seen metaphorically by Ferguson as a moment between a seed-time and a harvest, between the sowing of national feeling by Davis and the Young Ireland movement of the 1840s and the hoped-for fruits of independence indicated in the final stanza:

> O, brave young men, my love, my pride, my promise,
> 'Tis on you my hopes are set,
> In manliness, in kindliness, in justice,
> To make Erin a nation yet:
> Self-respecting, self-relying, self-advancing,
> In union or in severance, free and strong --

But when Ferguson himself died, some forty years later, in 1886, that hope was still unfulfilled. As now.

temporalities

It was about ten years after Ferguson's death, in 1895, that W. B. Yeats edited the book I was reading, *A Book of Irish Verse*, and included Ferguson's poem in it. In 1899 Yeats revised the volume, adding a few poems and a new Preface, dated August 15th 1899:

> One carries on the traditions of Thomas Davis . . not less than the traditions of good literature, which are the morality of a man of letters, . [even] . when one endeavours, as I have endeavoured in this book, to separate what has literary value from what has only a patriotic and political value, no matter how sacred it has become for us.

Yeats's anthology was reprinted a few times. The copy I was reading, this August morning, was printed in 1920. Most of the pages had remained uncut since the copy was bought and inscribed as a Christmas present in December 1920. I thought of that Christmas in Ireland, and of whoever had bought this present. Another moment in time, in history. Just before Christmas, on 23rd December 1920, the

Government of Ireland Act became law, giving statutory expression to the partition of Ireland into the Irish Free State and what we still think of as Northern Ireland.

Yeats had been thirty-five when he wrote that new preface in 1899, fifty-five by the time my 1920 copy was printed. And as I read it, this morning, Yeats himself has been dead for over fifty years. Ireland is still partitioned. But we no longer need to cut the leaves of newly published books. Some readers perhaps won't even know what that old-fashioned phrase even means, now.

Yeats' anthology *A Book of Irish Verse* is in its own way a history of Irish verse, a chronological selection, and therefore an assessment. It ends, in the second edition, in 1899. His own *Later Poems* begins from that same date, with selections from his 1899 volume *The Wind Among the Reeds*, situating himself into that history. My rather battered copy of *Later Poems* was published in December 1922, with a Preface dated 'Thoor Ballylee, May 1922':

> This book contains all poetry not in dramatic form that I have written between my seven-and-twentieth year and the year 1921.

In December 1921 the Anglo-Irish Treaty was finally signed. In May 1922 the first general election of the Irish Free State was being prepared. By December 1922, as my copy was printed, the Civil War was already intense and bitter. That copy too had remained unread till now.

later

So, I sat in my garden, through that sunny afternoon, reading *Later Poems*. For Yeats to call them 'Later Poems' is to assign them an odd temporal status, to put a shape on his life as falling into phases or periods. The poems thereby become curiously later than the moment in which they were actually written. To choose to include them is also to endorse thirty years of life, from twenty-seven to fifty-seven years of age. A history, a life held in the hand, read in a day, one August afternoon.

As I sat there, reading these poems of Yeats, that itself already felt like a historical gesture, a moment from a previous temporality, like cutting the pages of a book. Not just the occasional interruptions of the present, the telephone, an insistent transistor radio from somewhere distant. The very act of sitting peacefully and reading poetry in a garden seemed itself anachronistic, like a moment from someone else's past, or like a picture of someone reading.

On August 7th 1909 Yeats wrote a short poem in his journal which is now entitled 'Upon a House Shaken by the Land Agitation.' It was published in a newspaper in December that year. In 1922 he included it in *Later Poems*. I read it, there in the garden, nearly a century later and found it more moving than the Ferguson poem, though oddly like it, a kind of hypothetical lament. As if it were a lament for poetry itself.

A phrase from Walter Benjamin came to mind: 'The difficulty to be surmounted here consists in reading lyric poetry at all today.'

Here's the poem. How do you read it?

UPON A HOUSE SHAKEN BY THE LAND AGITATION

How should the world be luckier if this house,
Where passion and precision have been one
Time out of mind, became too ruinous
To breed the lidless eye that loves the sun?
And the sweet laughing eagle thoughts that grow
Where wings have memory of wings, and all
That comes of the best knit to the best? Although
Mean roof-trees were the sturdier for its fall,
How should their luck run high enough to reach
The gifts that govern men, and after these
To gradual Time's last gift, a written speech
Wrought of high laughter, loveliness and ease?

reading a poem

Walter Benjamin introduced his commentary on some poems by Bertolt Brecht with the remark:

> It is a known fact that a commentary is something different from a carefully weighed appreciation apportioning light and shade. The commentary proceeds from the classic nature of its text and hence, as it were, from a pre-judgement.

Yet he recognised that the very nature of a 'classic text' today may cloak a certain difficulty: 'The difficulty to be surmounted here consists in reading lyric poetry at all today.' Benjamin's own approach to Brecht's poems emphasised that the poems themselves 'have their pedagogical effect first, their political effect second and their poetic effect last of all' and the purpose of his commentary was 'to advance the pedagogical effect as much as possible and to retard the poetic one.'

What if I deliberately retard any 'poetic effect' of Yeats's poem, forget for a time that I am 'reading poetry'? What if I slow down my response and judgement, my more or less trained and automatic critical reaction to it, and ask, without too hasty a prejudgement, what it might mean for me.

Another voice might help, that of Mikhail Bakhtin. A rough working note from his later years:

> I call meaning the answers to the questions. That which does not answer any question is devoid of meaning for us ... Meaning always answers some questions.

Or, similarly, the voice of Voloshinov, from 1929:

> All true understanding is active and already represents the embryo of an answer. All understanding is dialogical. Understanding is opposed to utterance as one reply is oppposed to another within a dialogue.

Yeats's poem, after all, takes the form of questions: 'How should the world be luckier . . ?' 'How should their luck run high enough to reach . .?' If understanding this text involves an answer, the embryo of a reply, what would count as an answer or reply to those questions? And whose, we might also ask, are the questions, who asks for a reply?

Bakhtin, in a longer, difficult, note:

> The utterance (the verbal work) as non-reiterative whole, historically unique and individual . . . The entities of language studied by linguistics are by definition reproducible in an unlimited number of utterances [whereas] the entities of verbal communication—whole utterances—are non-reproducible (though they can be quoted) and are bound among themselves by dialogic relations. . . a reproduction is of course possible for a text (a reprinting for example); but the reproduction of a text by a subject (return to the text, new reading, new performance, citation) is a new and non-reiterative event in the life of the text, a new link in the historical chain of verbal communication.

I can indeed reproduce Yeats's poem, have it reprinted in this text, for example, and I can also invite you, as my reader, to read it. But does an understanding, an answer, a reply, rest upon and respond to a unique, non-repeatable utterance posed long ago, written in 1909? Is it that to which I am inviting myself, and you. to respond? Or does this text also invite, even necessitate, some form of reply to a question not simply 'quoted' but actually posed 'now', as I now sit at my desk to write and as you, or I, read or 'perform' those questions reproduced before us? Does understanding this text involve 'a new reading, a new performance' now, and therefore an answer to a question posed now? But what would be the question?

Bakhtin again:

> In no instance is the extra-verbal situation only an external cause of the utterance; it does not work from the outside

> like a mechanical force. On the contrary, the situation enters into the utterance as a necessary constitutive element of its semantic structure.

This is difficult to understand. We might readily accept that whatever the text meant for Yeats in 1909 involved some reference to his own situation. But in what sense can our understanding of it now involve a reference to our own situation now (whenever 'now' is for any particular reader)? The 'extra-verbal situation' of my citing this text now includes, among other things, my writing this and you reading it, now. How can that be involved in the very 'understanding' of Yeats's text? What question, and what embryo of an answer, is thereby involved, for us both?

relevant historical facts

First, another voice, perhaps more familiar. T. S Eliot in 1919:

> *Qua* work of art, the work of art cannot be interpreted; there is nothing to interpret; we can only criticise it according to standards, in comparison to other works of art; and for 'interpretation' the chief task is the presentation of relevant historical facts which the reader is not assumed to know.

What if we accept this advice of T.S. Eliot, from his essay on *Hamlet*, and try, conscientiously, to equip ourselves with some 'relevant historical facts'?

If I consult that pedagogical standby, *A Commentary on the Collected Poems of Yeats*, by Professor A. N. Jeffares, I find, it seems, at least two historical facts offered as relevant to this poem: a note on line 1:

> *this house*: Coole Park, Lady Gregory's house in County Galway, now demolished

and a note on line 10:

> *the gifts that govern men*: Sir William Gregory (1817-92), Lady Gregory's husband, a politician, had served as Governor of Ceylon.

Do these notes help our understanding? Do they modify my still embryonic reply? Not yet, I think. We need to supplement these facts. From another shelf I take down the *Dictionary of National Biography* and find a 'Sir William Gregory'.

'Sir William Gregory (1776 -1840)' —but from those dates I can see that this one is not the Sir William Gregory who interests me, but his grandfather. I note that from 1812 to 1831 this Sir William Gregory was first Civil and then both Civil and Military Under-Secretary of State to the Lord Lieutenant of Ireland. In other words, for some nineteen years (including the year when the later Sir William was born) he was close to being the effective Governor of Ireland. He was also, I note from a cross reference, the youngest son of Robert Gregory (1727-1810) who, among other accomplishments and positions, was once the Chairman of the East India Company—in other words, close to being the effective ruler of quite a large part of India. Finally, in the first *Supplement* to the *DNB*, I find the right Sir William Gregory. Born 1817. Educated Harrow. Christchurch, Oxford. Travel. Then an illuminating paragraph:

> He had up to this time taken no serious interest in politics; but in the spring of 1842 he was induced to stand as the Conservative candidate for Dublin. . . The election cost £9,000, of which the chief item was a 'gratification for 1500 freemen at £3 per head.'

So, at twenty-five, Sir William Gregory was Conservative Member of Parliament for Dublin. His income at that time, I discover, was some £7,000 a year, derived from the Coole Park estate and other sources. He could clearly afford to buy the seat, though in the light of that generous 'gratification' the phrase 'Gifts that govern men' perhaps takes on an ironic tinge.

Sir William remained MP for Dublin from 1842 to 1847. Interesting years, the years of the Great Famine. The *Dictionary of National Biography* does not tell me what the M.P. for Dublin did during the Great Famine. So I consult some other works.

gifts that govern men

A few paragraphs from an official record of the Famine, in the *Census of Ireland*, 1851, Part V:

> Generally speaking, the actually starving people lived upon the carcasses of diseased cattle, upon dogs, and dead horses, but principally upon the herbs of the field, nettle tops, wild mustard, and water cresses, and even in some places dead bodies were found with grasses in their mouth. . . . along the coast every description of seaweed was generally devoured, often with fatal consequence.
>
> It is scarcely possible to exaggerate in imagination what people will and are forced to do before they die from absolute want of food . . . Thus a stipendiary magistrate stated in Galway in extenuation of the crime of a poor prisoner brought up for stealing food, that to his own knowledge, before he was brought to the theft, he and his family had actually consumed part of a human body lying dead in the cabin with them.

John Pomfret quotes these paragraphs in his *The Struggle for Land in Ireland*, published in 1930. He gives a concise summary of the government's response to the famine in 1847:

> . . . several acts were passed providing for the expenditure of large sums of money on public works such as roads, piers, and so forth. At one time, March 1847, 734,000

> labourers were employed on relief works. This meant in all the support of three million persons, a considerable percentage of the population.
>
> The government brought this extravagant system of relief to a close during the months of March to August 1847. It fell back upon the very simple solution of feeding the poor. To this end the Poor Law had to be amended to permit of outdoor relief. Soup kitchens were erected in the impoverished districts and proved adequate to cope with the situation at a remarkably low cost.
>
> Unfortunately, there was attached a severe test, known as the Gregory Clause, which provided that no person in possession of more than a quarter acre of land could be deemed destitute and that it was not lawful for guardians to relieve such persons. . . Although provision was later made for the members of families evicted under such circumstances, the Gregory Clause has ever been condemned as 'the cheapest and most efficient of the ejectment acts.' For this reason and for others, evictions flourished during the period; from 1847-1849 there were 25,700 ejectments granted by the courts; while during four following years, 1849-1852, 58,423 families comprising 306,120 souls were evicted.

So that was what the M.P. for Dublin did during the Famine. Pomfret's account, published over fifty years ago, is perhaps dated. More sophisticated and better-documented accounts and explanations of the Great Famine have appeared since; many judgements might require revision. But even amid the statistics, tables, and graphs of a highly technical economic analysis published a few years ago by a leading cliometrician, Joel Mokyr's *Why Ireland Starved: a quantitative and analytical history of the Irish economy, 1800 - 1850*, I find a rare flash of human anger: 'such atrocities', he writes, 'as the Gregory Clause.'

Malcolm Brown, in his *The Politics of Irish Literature* (1972) has already drawn attention to the Gregory Clause in connection with Yeats's poetry:

> This clause which forced peasant clearances on a national rather than piece-meal scale . . was named the 'Gregory Clause' after its author, member for Dublin, Sir William Gregory of Coole Park, county Galway—the future husband in his old age of a young neighbour girl, Augusta Persse, known to us as Lady Gregory. Sir William's autobiography, edited by Lady Gregory, devotes a page or two of comment to the incident, quoting with approval the opinion of the *Dublin University Magazine* that the Gregory Clause had put an end to the two paramount hardships of the famine, namely 'the absorption by undeserving persons of a large portion of the public funds' and a poor rate that 'in many cases' had risen above 'the yearly rent of the land.' Sir William Gregory added that only nine of the hundred-odd Irish members had voted against the Gregory Clause, and that O'Connell's son had voted for it. 'Old Archbishop MacHale never forgave me on account of it,' he said. 'But it pulled up suddenly the country from falling into the open pit of pauperism on the verge of which it stood. Though I got an evil reputation in consequence, those who really understood the condition of the country have always regarded this clause as its salvation.'

Brown comments:

> Sir William's imperturbability should be kept in mind when interpreting Yeats's acid lines about those ungrateful farmers who carried off the stonework of some great manor house to 'patch the pig pen.'

Is Brown right and should we also keep in mind the Gregory Clause, and its effects, as a 'relevant historical fact' when reading Yeats's lines:

Although
Mean roof trees were the sturdier for its fall,
How should their luck run high enough to reach
The gifts that govern men..?

Some readers might find such 'historical facts' wholly irrelevant in their response to the poem. Others might be revulsed by the facts and their response to the poem accordingly diminished.

But what if Sir William was, after all, correct in claiming that 'those who really understood the condition of the country' have always regarded the Gregory Clause as its salvation?

theories of development

A passage from a marxist historian might also be kept in mind. Robert Brenner, writing on the origins of capitalist development, in *New Left Review*, number 104, argues as follows:

> Only where labour has been separated from possession of the means of production, and where labourers have been emancipated from any direct relation of domination (such as slavery or serfdom), are both capital and labour power 'free' to make possible their combination at the highest possible level of technology. Only where they are free, will such combinations appear feasible and desirable. Only where they are free, will such combinations be necessitated. . . Only under such a system, where both capital and labour power are thus commodities . . is there the necessity of producing at the 'socially necesssary' labor time in order to survive, and to surpass this level of productivity to ensure continued survival.

Brenner quotes Marx himself: 'So-called primitive accumulation, therefore, is nothing else than the historical process of divorcing the producer from the means of production.'

In other words, in certain circumstances, divorcing the farmer from his farm, the peasant from his land. Brenner and Marx had mainly in mind the transitional period from 'feudalism' to 'capitalism'. But an American economic historian, Barbara Solow, writing specifically on 19th century Ireland, in her *The Land Question and the Irish Economy, 1870 - 1903*, published in 1971, seems to endorse the same general argument, but from the apparently opposite perspective of classical *laissez-faire* economic theory:

> . . . the Famine and its aftermath were case studies in the application of classical remedies. The decline in population and the emigration and consolidation the classical economists preached all occured. By important legislative enactments . . barriers to the freer movement of capital were removed, and free trade in land was facilitated. The over-population spectre had departed and the feudal aspects of the law had been replaced: in the classical scheme, economic growth ought now to have taken place. . . In fact, economic growth did take place . . but progress was limited in two ways. First, in important parts of the country the over-population problem was not solved; pre-Famine conditions still persisted and population pressed on subsistence in the old way . . More important was the limitation on landlords' investment because of tenants' customary tenure rights. There was profit to be made in Irish agriculture and there was English capital ready to exploit it, but not on terms the Irish tenant would accept. Holdings would have to be re-arranged, techniques altered, and there was no place in this scheme for all the Irish tenants to remain on their tiny old family farms.

Solow is here summarising the conclusions of her (then) radically revisionist account of the 19th century Irish land struggle. As against the three-point programme pursued by the Land League—to extend the 'Ulster custom' of fixity of tenure, fair rent, and free sale of 'tenant rights' (the three F's)—she assembles convincing data to show that security of tenure had already obtained in practice at least from the

1850s, that actual rents were already generally lower than market value (the valuation base-line had been established in the rock-bottom year of 1849-50), and that 'tenant right' was already in operation as a form of saleable lease.

Thus, one could argue, the 1880s campaign for the three F's as a programme for redressing alleged grievances was singularly misplaced, while as a remedy for agricultural backwardness it was deeply misguided, since it was not in any case the 'Ulster custom' which had created the conditions for relative prosperity in the North; what was fundamentally needed throughout the country was to create the conditions for 'improvement' and for capital accumulation by landlords— and those conditions were not fixity of tenure but on the contrary the power to evict; not the obligation to pay tenants for their own local improvements but the power to rationalise the overall productivity of large estates without restriction by 'tenant rights'.

Sir William's infamous clause could, on this argument, be seen as enabling precisely that necessary process of abolishing 'tiny old family farms' and of fostering 'the historical process of divorcing the producer from the means of production', furthering the accumulation of capital necessary for the development of Irish agricultural productivity. Or is this to forget those dying generations?

As it happens, however, the Gregory Clause itself may not be the only 'relevant historical fact' involved in an assessment of that phrase 'the gifts that govern men'. Sir William Gregory's own later career, for example, took an unexpected turn. By 1865 he was no longer a Conservative but a Liberal M.P. and in 1866 introduced the first (unsuccessful) Bill in favour of tenant security and land purchase. He supported the Land Acts of 1870 and 1871, arguing that 'one of the greatest evils of Irish society' is 'that the great mass of the agricultural population should be divorced from all ownership in the soil.' By then he had sold off two-thirds of the Coole Park estate (mainly to pay gambling debts) and had offered his own tenants the right to purchase.

In other words, Sir William himself had moved to favouring the kind of programme Solow sees as economically inappropriate. Moreover, as it happens, it was his relative through marriage, Captain John Shaw-Taylor, a nephew of Lady Gregory, who convened the 1902 Land Conference, the direct precursor and begetter of the 1903 Wyndham Act which capped the series of Land Acts from 1870 onwards and enabled a massive transfer of land from landlords to former tenants, creating a widespread 'peasant proprietorship'. One of the stimuli for the 1903 Act was a provision of the 1881 Act which allowed the periodic adjustment downwards of rents, and it was in fact the workings of this provision which provided the occasion for Yeats's poem. Immediately after the draft of the poem in the Journal he noted:

> I wrote this on hearing the results of reductions of rent made by the courts.

Denis Donoghue, editor of Yeats's *Journal* adds:

> Fifteen tenants of the Gregory estate in Coole Park applied to the Land Court to have their rents reduced. The Land Commissioner, the Hon. Gerald Fitzgerald, granted their application, reducing the rents by approximately twenty per cent. Judgment was given on 30 July 1909. At the same time the Land Purchase Act of 1909 and certain provisions of the Finance Bill of 1909 imposed new burdens of taxation upon Irish landowners; notably the Increment Value Duty and the Reversion Duty.

The ironies do not cease there. Pomfret concluded his book with a chapter discussing the Wyndham Act, under the title 'The Solution of the Problem'. He saw Wyndham's 'great Act' as finally meeting the wishes and demands of the Land Leaguers. Yet within months of the passing of the Act, Michael Davitt—organiser and theorist of the Land League—in the final chapters of his own book *The Fall of Feudalism in Ireland* (1904) had already castigated the 1902 conference and the 1903 Act for, in effect, allowing the landlords a vastly inflated price for their land and a continuing massive subsidy from the British government and Irish tax-payer:

> . . the terms secured for the owners . . represented the re-conquest . . of almost all that the land movement and the land acts had won during the preceding twenty years for those tenants who had not bought their holdings.

The most obvious effect of the Wyndham Act, and subsequent amendments, was to create a large stratum of medium-sized owner-occupied farms (by 1922 'some 400,000 new owners were in possession of 13,000,000 acres of land', according to Pomfret) which, it could be argued, would have exactly the opposite effect from that hoped for in Brenner's schema: what such a redistribution constructed was a formidably entrenched barrier to fully capitalist development in Ireland.

Sinn Fein

In 1977 Sinn Fein: The Workers' Party (known then to the British media as 'the Official IRA') published its economic programme, which incorporated a great deal of revisionist research in its section on 'The Road to Underdevelopment'. The history of the 19th century land struggle is re-written to recognise a three-fold struggle, not only between 'tenants' and 'landlords' but between landlords, tenants and agricultural labourers and also between larger and smaller farm-owners. Since Sinn Fein economic documents are sometimes hard to find in British libraries, some passages of this analysis are worth quoting at length:

> Between 1845 and 1910 the number of labourers dropped from 700,000 to 300,000. The number of cottiers dropped from 300,000 to 62,000 in the same period. The number of farmers in the small farmer class (5 - 15 acres) dropped in the period between the Famine and the Great War from 310,000 to 154,000. But in this period, the number of farmers with more than 15 acres rose from 277,000 to

304,000. This class therefore had added 27,000 to their numbers, sharing out the spoils of those who had gone.

But, as the viable farm acreage rose from 15 acres in the nineteenth century to 30 acres in the 1930s to 40 acres in the 1950s and in our own time stands at 100 acres, so inevitably the bottom stratum is forced out and the class at the top becomes smaller in numbers while disposing of greater concentrations of land.

Ireland after the Famine entered fully into the normal mainstream of capitalist relations in agricultural production. This meant that all of Marx's predictions about the relationship between town and country would now take their inevitable course in the material lives of the Irish people. . . . Peasant life with its closed-in subsistence preoccupations is replaced by production for an open market system. This involves the rise of capitalist agriculture or what the IFA [Irish Farmers Association] calls 'commercial farming' . . the full scale production of food, not as a commodity to be consumed or exchanged for other commodities, but as a commodity to be exchanged for a profit

While the Famine of 1847 could have been alleviated in terms of human suffering if all the food produced was allowed to remain in Ireland through a relaxation of the laws of capitalist economics, there was no fundamental cure except fewer people on the land . . in some rural areas there was a density of 400 people per square mile and in the country as a whole there was an average of 335 people for every square mile of arable land. . . Ireland with a weak and incompetent bourgeoisie had neither towns, cities nor jobs that might have absorbed those forced to take the emigrant ship.

Today as economical farm holdings approach the hundred acre mark the same spectacle of enforced emigration faces 100,000 transitional small farmers. Now as in 1847 a

> temporary alleviation of misery provides neither a long term nor even a compassionate alternative.

In this recognition that the only basis for a solution in 1847 was a drastic reduction in the number of small farmers and peasant holdings, Sinn Fein seems to offer a retrospective, if partial, endorsement of the economic effects of that 'moral atrocity', the Gregory Clause.

problems of response

But is it really the case that involved in our response to the phrase 'gifts that govern men' is an answer, however embryonic, to questions about the economic causes and consequences of the Great Famine? In arriving at the 'reply' we would give to the questions of this poem are we indeed obliged—at whatever level of implicit comprehension and judgement—to decide what the economic development of Ireland could, or should, have been?

I suspect that in most readers, as in myself, there will be a certain resistance to that notion, a resistance worth making explicit. One immediate response might be that even if problems of development economics were allowed as, however remotely, 'relevant' to our response to this poem, most of us are not equipped to assess those problems. Relatively few readers of Yeats will have also read, say, the thousand or so publications on Irish economic and social history which appear, on average, every five years, or have the training necessary to assess, or even to understand, the equations and statistical correlations of Joel Mokyr's econometric analysis.

Nor is this only a matter of our lacking sufficient knowledge as individuals. If we try to understand what the effects of the Famine were, we might have to recognise that, in the words of one authority, J. M. Goldstrom:

> Scholars are at present confronted with a voluminous and contradictory mass of information when trying to quantify underlying trends in the pre-Famine era. . . Were farmers

> producing potatoes, cereals, pigs, butter and eggs in increasing quantities right up to 1845 rather than switching to beef and sheep? How far had subdivision progressed before the Famine? Was the population rising at a steady rate up to 1845? How far was it affected by emigration? What was happening to the age at marriage and to the marriage rate?

Moreover, as Goldstrom points out, though a mass of 19th century statistical data exists, historians are increasingly conscious of the 'treacherous nature of the data'. He lists some of the deficiencies, confusions, inconsistencies in the very material upon which any economic history has to be constructed. 'Nor should it be assumed', he writes, 'that collectors of data in these various areas of statistics were necessarily disinterested'. For example, Census officials in 1841 were, apparently, paid according to the number of people they could include, while respondents to inquiries about income may well, as always, have had the future attentions of tax collectors in mind. Nor should it be assumed, one might add, that more recent historians are necessarily disinterested either.

While it may be comparatively easy to recognise, retrospectively, that the writing of 'Irish history' during, say, 1800 to 1850 was deeply inflected by religious and ideological allegiances, it may be equally necessary but more difficult to acknowledge the same factors at work in more recent and apparently more objective modes of writing history. Finally, of course, it is inevitable and predictable that new historical research will soon overturn currently accepted conclusions, including the ones I have offered here.

These are, of course, familiar factors in the writing of any history and not peculiar to that of Ireland. Any resistance, therefore, to allowing inquiries into Ireland's economic history to influence our response to Yeats's poem may well claim to rest upon a sensible basis.

There is, however, a deeper level of resistance. I have deliberately, so far, quoted at length from a variety of 'sources' and 'authorities', rather than offered any brief summary of historical 'findings' or simply given a battery of bibliographical references. In providing those quotations I am aware that at least some of my readers will have experienced, let us say, a certain fluctuation of interest in following them, perhaps a quiet curiosity as I commented on the *DNB* entries on the Gregory family, then a mildly horrified response to the 1851 descriptions of the Famine, followed by perhaps a faintly impatient reading of the extracts from Pomfret, and finally a marked glazing of the eyes and suspension of attention for the passages from Brenner, Solow and Sinn Fein.

For if, as is likely, most of my (remaining) readers are students of 'literature' there may have been not only a lurking sense that such extracts are irrelevant, inappropriate or unnecessary, but also that the very modes of analysis they deploy are somehow unsympathetic, not the kind of writing we wish to be concerned with, a perhaps grudging acknowledgment that *someone* has to be engaged with such matters but a kind of relief that it need not be us. Alerted to a problem in the data available for constructing an economic history—for example, that Irish and English 'acres' were of a different size in the 19th century and it is not always clear in the massive detail of the 1845 Devon Commission report on Irish agriculture (a major 'source') which unit is being used —we, as readers of poetry or as literary critics, are only too happy to leave the resolution of such problems to professionals in remote disciplines. This is an understandable reaction, partly a matter of individual temperament, partly an unavoidable institutional division of labour.

But it is then worth curving these responses themselves back onto the phrase from the poem: 'gifts that govern men'. If we are, at whatever level and for whatever reasons, so reluctant or ill-equipped to confront the problems of deciding what the course of Irish economic development has or could have been, of tackling the genuine difficulties involved in judging the effects of an overall pattern of evictions upon the conditions for later development, then does not this very reluctance also preclude us from any justified assessment of Gregory's own responsibility in proposing the Gregory Clause?

If we still wish to judge Sir William Gregory's exercise of 'the gifts that govern men', must we not recognise that the kind of responsibility and decision involved in proposing responses to the 1847 famine included the kinds of difficulty in assessing economic theories and relations between cause and effect which we have shown ourselves as disinclined to engage with. In other words, we might have to recognise (to adapt and apply to ourselves another phrase from the poem) that our own 'gifts', or inclinations or skills or knowledge, do not 'run high enough' to reach some of those which we acknowledge are required to 'govern men'.

We might, of course, readily admit this in our actual lives, in our actual exercise of political responsibility, yet in reading Pomfret's or Brown's account of the Gregory Clause this may not have been our initial reaction at all. Once the connection was suggested between the Gregory Clause and Yeats's poem, the dominant response may have been, however *sotto voce*, a 'moral' judgement, exemplified by Mokyr's term 'moral atrocity'. Such a response would be in line with our normal sense of the kinds of claim 'poetry' makes upon us. But just as it may now be clearer that Eliot's notion of 'presenting relevant historical facts' is not as simple as it might have seemed, so it may also be increasingly more difficult to know just what is to count as an 'appropriate' response to the questions posed in this poem—once we take them seriously, 'retard the poetic effect', and treat those questions as posed now.

the extra-verbal situation

We can return at this point to Bakhtin's claim that the 'extraverbal situation', in every instance, 'enters into the utterance as a necessary element of its semantic structure.'

My own phrase, above, 'mildly horrified' is a case in point. To speak of a 'mildly horrified' response to the 1851 Census descriptions of the Famine might seem wierdly inept as well as oxymoronic: how could one be 'mildly' 'horrified'?

Yet when I originally wrote that phrase, for a lecture in Liverpool several years ago (writing too has its temporalities), the television news was daily presenting pictures of the extensive famine in Ethiopia and the Sudan, in 1985. With those vivid and immediate images before me of children actually dying of starvation as I wrote, my own response to the 1851 account of the Irish famine was both sharpened and dulled—a more acute sense of what that suffering must have been in 1847 and at the same time an awareness of its distance, its past-ness, even its relatively small scale (three million people) compared with the 1985 African famine (some 180 million people at risk), and compared also with all the other famines and catastrophes, horrors and brutalities, we have been made aware of during the past several decades. Insofar as the 'extraverbal situation' of all readers today includes such awareness, the phrase 'mildly horrfied' might remain apt. Even so, to introduce this element of the 'extra-verbal situation' explicitly may still be felt to break a received critical decorum.

There are, however, some familiar and accepted forms of appeal or reference, in critical discourse, to the critic's or reader's own position, their extra-verbal situation. T. R. Henn, introducing a Yeats Summer School in Sligo once offered an extended meditation on one such kind of appeal:

> That the Lake District should have fired so greatly Wordsworth's imagination, that Cowper's poetry and his hymns should be related to the placid and comfortable waters of the Ouse, that Crabbe's grim realism should spring from that 'bold surly savage race' that you still find around Aldeburgh [*sic*] — we take these for granted. . . But there is a world of difference between reading of the genius of place and meeting that genius face to face, with the words moving in our minds. When I first saw the Cave of the Cumaean Sybil, on the south of the little sandy bay where Aeneas landed from Troy, its many mouths were filled with German machine-guns sited to fire on the beach; and it took on a strange metaphysical dimension from them. To see the long-extinct volcano of

> Solfatera, where the ground rings hollow like a drum, with its pools of boiling mud, and to realise that you are walking on one of the classic entrances to Hell, is to understand, suddenly, something of Dante.

He ends his lecture:

> Perhaps, also, to understand fully these poems [by Yeats] one needs to have been born and bred in one of the Western Irish towns; to remember how it was the centre of your world, how the mountains and the river and the woods became a portion of your life forever; to have loved with a sense of possession even the roadside bushes where the cotters hung their clothes to dry. That sense of possession was the very centre of the matter. Elsewhere you are only a passer-by, for everything is owned by so many that it is owned by no-one.

One wonders whether the cotters shared quite the same 'sense of possession' about their bushes. But a Sligo itinerary for students attending the Summer School naturally followed from such an attitude:

> If we stand on the summit of Kocknaraea—and you must carry a stone with you on your climb to put on the Cairn, else you will have no luck afterwards—we can watch the scene and the centuries mirrored as in some kind of glass..
> … You will see from Drumcliffe the cliffs that lie to the North-West of the Mountain, over which a troop of cavalry were driven to their death . .
> …You can visit the great waterfall that plunges into the head of Ballisodare Bay, and remember that . .

This bringing into play of one's own knowledge of the Sligo countryside to illuminate one's response to Yeats's poems, or a reference to aspects of one's own upbringing in Ireland, may add an acceptably 'relevant' dimension to a critic's commentary, and indeed endow an Irish-born critic with a particular authority and privilege by comparison with readers who do not share that extra-verbal situation.

We can recognise this kind of allusion in many forms—a deployment of personal anecdote, of local memory, of appeal to specifically individual or shared group experience—in discussions of literature, though more normally in conversation than in print. But there are received or obvious limits to this kind of appeal in academic critical writing. We can suggest one limit by instancing a passage from another distinguished Yeats critic. Peter Ure, discussing Yeats's poem 'The Statues', offers this gloss upon the opening lines:

> Both the first and second stanzas of 'The Statues' deal, it would appear, with the 'Doric' sculptures of the fifth century: Pythagoras, of the sixth century, was the forerunner of the Phidian work. Yeats has much to say in *A Vision* about the historic significance of the differences between the archaic sculpture of the sixth century, and the Ionic and Doric modes; he read Furtwaengler and thought that the Ionic and Doric united in the work of Phidias. He makes none of these distinctions in the poem before us, and omits the idea . . that 'measurement' came after 'those riders upon the Parthenon'...

Ure's comment was first published in an article in the *Review of English Studies* in 1949. As it happens, we know from Frank Kermode's memoir of Ure that, only a few years before, Ure had himself recorded an impression of the Parthenon. After imprisonment in the early part of the war as a conscientious objector, Ure had finally enrolled in a Relief and Refugees team and in January 1945 joined his unit in Athens. Kermode assembles his account largely from Ure's own journal of that time:

> Greece was involved in a disastrous civil war, and British troops had returned there to oppose the revolutionary organisation ELAS. Ure records that on his arrival 'Athens has only been "cleared" of ELAS troops about ten days . . Up the Monastery hill (where live Virgins and Saints covered in thick silver) which was formerly held by ELAS are Vickers machine-gun bands and other relics . . This ammunition is British ammunition used against the

> British.' In the museum at the Diplyon, among many untouched objects, 'a large figure-painted amphora lying drastically smashed inside its glass case.' . . Back in the streets a strange smell issued from buildings wrecked in the recent street fighting. 'They say it emanates from corpses in the basements choked with rubble. They are putting quicklime down.' . . 'Athens stands revealed as a dreary and even evil town,' he wrote on 25 January 1945, 'and the Acropolis and Parthenon a grim joke.' He greatly disliked the police, who, having worked with the Italians and Germans, were now gaoling ELAS anti-Fascists on behalf of the British government.

A simple juxtaposing of those two passing references to the Parthenon, in Ure's 1945 journal and in his 1949 article, might provide no mutual illumination whatsoever. The Parthenon, obviously, has a wider and more permanent cultural significance than any individual and temporary reaction to it, and it is Yeats's use of that significance which Ure tries to clarify in his critical gloss on 'The Statues'. We might assume that Ure's own interest in the poem could have been modified by his experience of Greek art *in situ*, but it would be regarded as somewhat eccentric or self-indulgent to introduce such personal associations into a critical argument.

We might speculate that Ure's response to other poems by Yeats, for example 'Upon a Political Prisoner' or 'Meditations in Time of Civil War', could have been shadowed by, and illuminated by, Ure's own experiences as a conscientious objector in Walton Gaol and Wormwood Scrubs, or by his observation of the 'civil war' in Greece in 1945. As far as I know, however, no explicit traces of any such personal resonances ever intrude upon Ure's published criticism of Yeats. According to critical decorum of the period, we would not expect it.

But what if we notice a broader parallelism of situation: between the role of the British Army in Greece after the Second World War, as it would have been perceived by an ELAS intellectual (several of whom Ure encountered in British gaols), and the role of the British Army in Ireland after the First World War, and before? Particularly perhaps as a conscientious objector, Ure could well have recognised that his reaction to the Parthenon in the conditions of 1945 — 'a grim joke' — was not simply an idiosyncratic response but one deeply indicative of moral strains, clashes of received values, a density and complexity of doubts and dilemmas, embedded in the structure of the situation in which he found himself. Any member of the British forces, even one attached to a Refugees Mission, could well have had any unease about his own role reinforced by a thoughtful reading of Yeats's poems at that time.

Yet for Ure to have brought any of that awareness into his critical writings on Yeats, as a way of confronting the complexity of Yeats's own responses, would certainly have involved him in a very different kind of relation to the readers of the *Review of English Studies*, a different kind of writing. The general experience of war, and in many cases of active service, was in 1949 a shared, if unstated, reference point for a whole generation of literary critics and readers in England: Henn's memory of the Cumaean cave bristling with German machineguns is one tiny, casual instance. Ure's 1949 article concludes with a quotation from Yeats that must have had a resonance at that time which no longer obtains in the same way for younger readers today:

> 'As life goes on,' Yeats wrote in *The Trembling of the Veil*, 'we discover that certain thoughts sustain us in defeat, or give us victory . . and it is these thoughts, tested by passion, that we call convictions.'

It was, and is, rare for a literary critic to explain the relation between any specific personal experience and an offered interpretation of a poem. William Empson's references to how his understanding of Milton's *Paradise Lost* was modified by his experiences in China during the 1949 revolution is one of the memorable exceptions. Raymond Williams's work provides others. And some feminist criticism has begun to make this more possible.

But it is worth asking whether the characteristic exclusion from professional literary criticism of the explicitly personal and specific dimension of response has not helped to sever the practice of literary analysis and commentary from the ways in which readers do actually read poems. A poem often takes on an intensity and significance for us when it is most associated with individual resonances and applications, yet the curiously impersonal mode of writing developed in professional literary criticism precludes attention to this. Whatever the unstated personal resonance or implicit shared concerns and experiences of a generation of readers, the accepted job of the critic has been to focus upon the poem primarily at its point of production—what it meant when it was written—and only in a derivative and more general way upon the point of its reception, with reference not to a specific reader but to 'any' reader, a response possible in principle for anyone, a 'universal meaning'. An awareness of, for example, specifically gendered responses has only relatively recently begun to modify and challenge this basic assumption.

the Liverpool connection

There is, however, another aspect of the 'extra-verbal situation' which 'enters into the utterance' in a different way from either a specifically individual or a generational or gendered resonance. The case of Ure's possible reaction to Yeats's poems while serving with the British Army in Greece has perhaps indicated a sense in which the 'extra-verbal situation' of both poet and reader might be both structurally consonant and in a certain historical continuity. By pursuing further the links between Sir William Gregory and the Famine we can illustrate—no more than that, yet—that further aspect in relation to 'Upon a House'.

In my own case, for example, the causes and effects of Irish emigration in the later 19th century are of considerable personal interest, since the history of my own home city, Liverpool, was deeply and permanently shaped by successive waves of Irish immigration. I might also remark at this point that the Liverpool in which I grew up had, at one time, been the hub of a truly global transport and trade network, not least the trade in slaves, and that I took it for granted that I had aunts in Ceylon and Chicago, uncles in Nigeria and Australia, that the merchant navy side of the family had sailed in the Caribbean and the South China Seas, the Mediterranean and the Baltic, and that my Irish grandmother had postcards on her sideboard from Montevideo and Rome as well as from Dublin and Cork.

In April 1847 Irish refugees from the Famine were arriving in Liverpool at the rate of 3,000 a day. In one of the later waves my own great-grandparents arrived. The issue for me, then, is not only how far my response to that poem and to that phrase is or should be influenced by a knowledge of such historical facts, but more fundamentally that my very existence to have any responses at all is consequent upon that history. If Henn's birth in Sligo gave him a privileged relation to Yeats's poems, my own birth in Liverpool gives me another definite, if less privileged, relation.

At a more general level, indeed, the present conditions of existence of almost all my likely readers—English, Irish, American—have been deeply and permanently affected by that same history. Consider, for example, the following brief remarks on American economic history, by Charles Post:

> Prior to the 1840s . . the restricted size of the available labour force posed problems for industrial capital, especially in cotton textile production. In the 1840s and 1850s the obstacle to the development of capitalism posed by the shortage of labour power was overcome by massive emigration from Europe. While immigration had taken place in the 1820s and 1830s, its volume was so small as to have little impact on the supply of labour power to capital. In the 1840s the volume of immigration tripled, and doubled again in the 1850s. The commercial crisis of the mid-1840s, the potato famine in Ireland, and the active recruitment of immigrant workers by industrial capital produced this increase in the numbers of immigrants to the US in the twenty years prior to the Civil War. This

massive inflow of workers . . created the first permanent reserve army of labour in the US.

The chain of effects we could trace here, from the Gregory Clause evictions to US immigration to the development not only of US capitalism but of all those familiar Irish factors in US politics, would—of course—be highly selective, partial, tendentious; it would clearly be absurd to trace the global domination of American power back to the M.P. for Dublin in 1847.

And yet, not wholly untrue or irrelevant. For the role of the Gregory family in governing Ireland, India and Ceylon is most certainly part of that process of complex causes and responsibilities which has shaped our present world.

Even so, surely—one has to say—all this, however remotely or minimally or truistically 'true', is irrelevant to how we read this poem. It has no purchase upon our actual response, and even if, by some perverse over-sensitivity, it did have some influence for a peculiar reader, it surely should not have. We might accept that the topographical characteristics of a known territory may shape our understanding of a work of art. We might even be prepared to accept that a particular individual experience may influence a reader's response to a poem — though we would, normally, it often seems, still prefer to see critical analysis formulated in terms of some putatively shared 'human nature'. But the notion that a shared global history is more than a background context to any particular reading is surely stretching a point. Perhaps.

And perhaps it is time to read the poem again. Especially the first line:

How should the world be luckier if this house ...?

how should the world

Professor Jeffares's *Commentary* offered as a 'relevant historical fact' that Sir William Gregory had served as

Governor of Ceylon. With the phrase 'gifts that govern men' still in mind, it is worth reading Elizabeth Coxhead's account, in her biography of Lady Gregory, of how Sir William became Governor of Ceylon in 1872:

> He knew now that the great political positions would elude him, and after the passing of the Second Reform Bill he began to look around for a change of occupation. A colonial governorship would, he felt, suit, and he fixed on Ceylon, perhaps because [his friend] Layard's cousin Charles was already high in the legislature there. He spoke to Lady Waldegrave, a powerful political hostess who was his friend, 'and she at once, and successsully, betook herself to obtain the promise of it from Lord Granville'; it was as simple as that.

Indeed. Coxhead's own judgement is that:

> As Governor he was in every way a success. . . He started the building of the great breakwater which was to turn Colombo into a major port, he repaired the irrigation system, widened the roads, reduced the drinking shops, established small rural dispensaries on the Irish system of medical relief.

We should perhaps supplement her observations with the references to Sir William's governorship in the *History of Ceylon*, edited by K. M. de Silva and written by Sri Lanka scholars after independence. There aren't very many references to Sir William in the substantial volume. A sample:

> . . Gregory decided to settle this vexed question [of chena lands] once and for all through a survey settlement . . Though he and his advisers realised that the settlement would take time, they were blithely unaware of the magnitude of the task. . . Attempts to survey individual chena plots proved too costly and difficult. A scheme of block surveys . . was tried and discarded. They eventually adopted a system of surveying the boundaries of lands

> that were claimed by private parties while sketching in individual claims within these blocks by hand. . . When the day for implementing these agreements arrived, however, many proprietors would not give up their plots . . And the governor had no legal power to enforce the settlement. This impasse brought an early end to Gregory's survey settlement scheme. And there the matter lay.
>
> . . Governor Sir William Gregory, a man of pronounced liberal outlook, lent his support to a the campaign for disestablishment [of the Anglican church in Ceylon] in the years 1876-7. But his impetuosity and tactlessness nullified his efforts and it was left to Governor Sir James Longden to effect the disestablishment in 1881.
>
> . . In the 1870s a change was observed. This began with Governor Gregory who displayed an active interest in Buddhism, and in oriental learning. By making a contribution to the repair of the Ruvanveli Dagaba at Anurandhapura, and the gift of two lamps to the Dalada Maligava in Kandy, Gregory demonstrasted a courteous regard for Buddhism.
>
> . . It was Gregory, once again, who boldly reversed the attitude discernible since the Great Rebellion of 1817-1818, of being wary of the power and privileges of the Kandyan aristocracy. . . Where Gregory was driven by sentiment and impulse, Gordon was purposeful in his policy of an aristocratic revival.
>
> . . Even Governor Gregory, despite his strong Liberal inclinations, and his initiation of reform in every other sphere, remained unenthusiastic over the liberalisation of the constitution. On the contrary, he was an unabashed advocate of the need for conserving and strengthening the powers of the governor.

We could add a few more passages, and there are other accounts, by non-Sri Lankans. But on balance it would seem that the historians of the people whom he governed have a somewhat less enthusiastic appreciation of Sir William's governorship than his wife's biographer.

And in any case our assessment of his exercise of 'the gifts that govern men' may well be influenced by our reactions to the very fact of his exercising them in Ceylon at all.

A very brief reminder may be useful of some salient aspects of Ceylonese history in the 19th century:

> Once the Dutch had been evicted, London proceeded to complete the unfinished work left by Amsterdam. In 1815, the British fomented a revolt by the Kandyan aristocracy against the last Kandyan monarch and marched into the uplands to depose him at their request. Two years later, when the same nobility rose against British rule in a fierce rebellion . . they were crushed by the occupiers they had themselves invited into their remote redoubts. Subsequent risings in the 1820s and in 1848 were soon stamped out; a communications network was constructed to end the old inaccessibility of the uplands; and, for the first time, colonial rule now covered the whole island. The military and political preconditions had now been laid for a massive economic transmutation of the island.
>
> In the 1830s coffee was introduced into Ceylon, a crop which flourishes in high altitudes. Speculators and entrepreneurs from England swarmed to the new conquered uplands, and expropriated vast tracts of forest on the higher slopes of the Kandyan valleys from the villagers who had traditionally used them as common lands for fuel and fruit-gathering. The right to seize this land was 'purchased' from the British State at nominal price; it was then cleared and converted into enormously profitable coffee plantations.
>
> The Kandyan villagers refused to abandon their traditional subsistence holdings and become wage-workers on these new capitalist estates. . . An infamous system of contract labour was established, which transported hundreds of

thousands of Tamil 'coolies' from Southern India into Ceylon for the coffee estates. These Tamil labourers died like flies, both on the journey itself, and in the nightmarish conditions of the early plantations. Nearly 1,000,000 were imported in the 1840s and 1850s alone: the death rate was 250 per 1,000. The decimation and super-exploitation of this class founded the fortunes of British imperialism in Ceylon . . allowing the colonial state to manipulate and exacerbate ethnic antagonisms between Tamil and Sinhalese in a classic strategy of divide and rule.

The coffee economy collapsed in the 1870s, when a leaf disease ravaged the plantations. But the economic system it had created survived intact into the epoch of its successor crop. In the 1880s, tea was introduced on a wide scale and soon had ousted coffee completely . . Tea was more capital-intensive and needed a higher volume of initial capital to be processed. The result was that individual estate-owners were now supplanted by large English consolidated companies . . Monoculture was incrasingly capped by monopoly within the plantation economy. The pattern thus created in the 19th century has remained essentially identical ever since: Liptons and Brooke Bonds rule the Ceylonese massif down to this day.

As I copied that out, there were reports on the BBC news of large-scale fighting, murder, and reprisals between Tamils and Sinhalese in Sri Lanka. The newspapers recently carried accounts of the scandalous wages and inhuman conditions on the tea plantations. Liptons began, I believe, as an Irish-based firm. It says on the packet of a quarter of tea I bought at a Liptons super-market: 'Mountain grown from the tea gardens of the central hills of Sri Lanka (Ceylon).' When we read in Lady Gregory's autobiography that she owned a jewel-box which had belonged to the last Kandyan Queen, or in Coxhead's biography that 'four cultivated generations had filled' Coole Park 'with books, pictures, statuary, records and mementoes of wide travel' (that innocuous word 'travel'), perhaps we should recall Walter Benjamin's laconic remark: 'There is no cultural document that is not at the same time a record of barbarism.'

It would be possible to add to this material on Ceylon a brief account of, say, the role of the East India Company in the expansion of British imperial rule, paying particular attention to the rather murky part played by Sir William's great-grandfather, Robert Gregory, in the impeachment proceedings against Warren Hastings, thanks to which Gregory became Chairman of the Company —for three months—at a crucial moment of transition in 1872. But to add the history of India to the history of Ceylon would merely reinforce a point already apparent: that when Yeats's poem asks 'How should the *world* be luckier . .? ' there is a sense in which that is not an empty formulation. The history of the Gregory family is not simply that of some minor Galway gentry: several Gregorys had been actors on the stage of world history, in Ireland, India, Ceylon and, not least, as M.P.s in England itself. As Anglo-Irish members of the British ruling class—those who most decidedly 'governed'—the Gregorys could take a considerable portion of the planet, the 'world', as the arena for the exercise of their 'gifts', a fact not without its potential ironies and contradictions.

For example, both Sir William and Lady Gregory, while stopping over in Egypt in the 1880s, took a concerned interest in the fate of the Egyptian nationalist leader Arabi (should we here add a brief history of Egypt under British control?). Lady Gregory records two symptomatic encounters in her journal:

> *17th.* I met Arabi in the hall. I thanked him for the photograph he had sent me with the words 'Arabi the Egyptian; I present my picture to Lady Gregory as a souvenir to preserve friendship.' He has the Slave Trade suppression 'next to his heart' and he will carry it out.
>
> *19th.* At the Fitzgeralds. [She glosses this:] Mr (afterwards Sir Gerald) Fitzgerald was one of those with whom I carried on a good-humoured quarrel . . he did not lose his temper with us, though as a well-paid and well-meaning

> official he wished the Egyptian government left undisturbed. He would sometimes threaten to come in return and wave the green Land League flag at the gates of Coole.

In 1909 the Land Commissioner who ruled that the rents of the fifteen Coole Park tenants should be reduced by 20% was the Hon. Gerald Fitzgerald. An article on Arabi was Lady Gregory's first appearance in print.

Yeats's poem does not, we should remember, ask 'How should the lot of Irish peasants be improved?' or even 'How should Ireland be better off?'. It asks 'How should the world be luckier...?' If we were to attempt any serious reply to this direct question, including an assessment of the various exercises of the 'gift' of governing, would we not be involved in a rather curious process, that of assessing, and somehow judging, the history of the world? But how does one even attempt to judge world history?

Among the few attempts to do so that could be instanced, one is particularly apt, since it concerns British rule in India and touches upon some of the issues that have already engaged us in the history of Ireland, Ceylon, and the USA: land, population and the development of capitalism. It also occurs, as it happens, in a series of newspaper articles prompted by the Parliamentary debates on the impending expiration of the East India Company's charter in 1854. Writing for the *New York Daily Tribune*, Karl Marx first describes at length the systems of Indian agriculture and industry and then continues:

> English interference having placed the spinner in Lancashire and the weaver in Bengal, or sweeping away both Hindu spinner and weaver, dissolved these small, semi-barbarian, semi-civilised communities, by blowing up their economical basis, and thus produced the greatest, and, to speak the truth, the only social revolution ever heard of in Asia. . . England, it is true, in causing a social revolution in Hindustan, was actuated only by the vilest

> interests, and was stupid in her manner of enforcing them. But that is not the question. The question is, can mankind fulfil its destiny without a fundamental revolution in the social state of Asia? If not, whatever may have been the crimes of England, she was the unconscious tool of history in bringing about that revolution.

Characteristically, Marx concludes the article with a quotation from a poet:

> Then, whatever bitterness the spectacle of the crumbling of an ancient world may have for our personal feelings, we have the right, in point of history, to exclaim with Goethe:
>
> Should this torture then torment us
> Since it brings us greater pleasure?
> Were not through the rule of Timur
> Souls devoured without measure?

Others may feel less confident that 'we' have any 'right' 'in point of history' to endorse the application of Goethe's lines, or hesitate in accepting an overall schema or grand narrative of history in which global capitalist industrialisation is a necessary stage in human social advance.

However, one reason for uncertainty about making any such judgements might, quite simply, be the realisation that we do not know enough to frame or answer an approriate question. If I had myself to make an overall judgement on the British in India—and in Ceylon and in Egypt, in Burma and the Caribbean, in Kenya and Nigeria, in Malaysia and Palestine, in Cyprus and Greece . . —I certainly would feel the need to know a great deal more than I do. When that eminently conscientious Victorian, Friedrich Engels, set out to write a History of Ireland he intended to go back a long way:

> To understand the nature of the soil of present day Ireland we have to return to the distant epoch when the so-called Carboniferous System was formed.

[Several pages later:]

> It is obvious that Ireland's misfortune is of ancient origin; it begins directly after the carboniferous strata were deposited. A country whose coal deposits are eroded, placed near a larger country rich in coal, is condemned by nature to remain for a long time the farming country for the larger country when the latter is industrialised. That sentence, pronounced millions of years ago, was carried out this century.

Even when merely moving a motion at a committee meeting in favour of the 1867 Fenians, Marx prepared notes for a speech on Irish history since 1172 that, if delivered, would have lasted several hours.

Yet even if I were to display the same commendable passion for knowledge and understanding of overall historical processes as these two typically ambitious scholars, any attempt to offer a *judgement* upon that overall process would seem very odd, perhaps pointless. Could it really make sense to say that the history of the world *should* have been different?

Several answers are possible. One could, on the one hand, find plausible an attitude which quite definitely regarded the present overall state of the world as morally intolerable: a common enough reaction, after all, to those television news reports which juxtapose starving African childen with pictures of European food mountains. Yet, given such an attitude, trying then to assess the degree of moral responsibility, for the historical construction of that situation, of one Dublin M.P. for 1847, or even of several generations of Gregorys, would seem mildly absurd, an insane kind of disproportion.

Conversely, however, it might be just as plausible to offer a categorical moral judgement upon a specific action by an individual—that Gregory's 1847 Clause was a ''moral atrocity', whatever its alleged economic effects—yet to feel that any moral judgement upon the entire history of the world would be wholly ludicrous, a futile moral fantasy.

What both positions share, however, is the sense that in moving from the individual or local level to the global level the nature of the judgement we feel called upon to make changes in character. Certain kinds of judgement, and certain kinds of emotional reaction also, become less relevant, less applicable, as we move—in whichever direction—from one 'level' to another.

It might then be important to locate, if possible, the point at which that change in reaction occurs for us; to focus there might be illuminating, not only morally but perhaps strategically, suggesting not only a point of intersection or mediation between moral judgements but also a possible point of intervention.

For example, one familiar focus, or hinge, for overall historical analysis, for political and moral judgement, and for attempted intervention, has been 'class'. *The Economic Programme of Sinn Fein: The Workers Party*, in its polemical introduction, offers a familiar instance of this kind of combination of historical analysis and moral judgement upon a 'class'. Writing of the 'Irish National Bourgeoisie', the authors state:

> The first part of this book is a history of that greedy class. . . we follow its delinquent and retarded career . . from the end of the Penal Laws which gave it birth; follow its selfish infancy when it secured Catholic Emancipation at the expense of the mass of the population; observe it during the Great Famine, which saw it eat when others starved; watch its adolescent grabbing of the land of Ireland in the clearances that followed the Famine; study it in the prime of life, as from the Land Wars in the 1880s to its bloody triumph in the Civil War of 1922, it takes to itself the title of a 'national' bourgeoisie; chronicling its last senile and doomed efforts to buy another lifespan by selling the young and vigorous population it rules into the hands of American monopoly capital in our own day. All that mean and sordid history might have been redeemed in retrospect had the Irish bourgeoisie carried out the one

> essential task, which gives the capitalist class of any country the minimum right to survival. It refused to construct a healthy capitalism.

The continuous 'it', as a permanent agent of history somehow retaining its essential identity across several periods, might of course be compared with similar metaphorical individuals, having a birth, prime and decay: 'a nation once again", for example, or that peculiar entity called 'Great Britain'.

However, the formulation of the question in Yeats's poem remains stubbornly different: it does not ask, 'Would the history of the world have been morally or economically better if Sir William had exercised his gifts in a different way?'—though some version of that question may well influence our reaction to the poem. Nor does it ask, directly, about the doings of a whole class—though that may be the framework we assume it to operate within. Nor is its vocabulary, explicitly, that of morality at all. It actually asks a question we may find increasingly odd: How should the world be luckier if this house..?

if this house

Jeffares is more explicit than Yeats in naming the house of the poem as 'Coole Park, Lady Gregory's house in County Galway, now demolished.' He is, obviously, justified. Though Yeats never included the name 'Coole Park' in either the poem or its various titles, he clearly had Coole in mind. In *The Green Helmet and other poems* (1910) the title was, simply, "Upon a Threatened House", while on its first publication of all, in *McClure's Magazine* for December 1910, it was entitled 'To a Certain Country House in Time of Change'. So we are indeed being asked about a certain house, a specific building, a particular home: *this* house.

The house itself no longer exists, so we cannot include it in an actual itinerary, but there are various descriptions of it in print. We can sample a few:

From Joseph Hone's biography of Yeats, 1942:

> The unpretentious gates of Coole open on an avenue of great trees, their leafy embracing branches a tunnel of twilight on the sunniest day. The avenue curves through wood and fields to a modest, white-fronted house, rather like a large Italian farm-house, which looks across a wide sloping field to a great wood . . More woods spread out behind the house, the paths lost; at the confines of the demesne, in a landscape of mysterious and desolate beauty, as though one were at the world's end, lies a grey lake with wild swans . . At Coole Yeats found a life of order and labour where all outward things were the signatures of an inward life. . . Many generations, and no uncultured generation, had left images of their service in the outlines of wood and fields at Coole, in sculptures and pictures, in furniture, in a fine library with editions of the classics and books on plants and agriculture.

From Elizabeth Coxhead's biography of Lady Gregory:

> Coole was a pleasure house, a Sleeping Beauty palace in a thick forest. For by his plantations the East India chairman, homesick perhaps for Asia, had created an artificial jungle, quite against the grain of that limestone country. His descendants had inherited his passion for tree-planting. . . The drive was two miles long, and the last mile was first an arching avenue of ilex, then a twisting forest track. The house itself disappointed many . . by its architectural poverty. It was an oblong white Georgian building with a plain little porch, the counterpart of hundreds in Ireland. The principal living-rooms, library, and drawing room, looked the other way, west towards the lake, through undistinguished but serviceable bays. All the house's distinction lay within. Four cultivated generations had filled it with books, pictures, statuary, records and mementoes of wide travel, all bearing the imprint of personal taste and personal achievement. It was the house of people who had never been afraid to use their brains.

From T.H.S. Escott's biography of Anthony Trollope, 1913:

> There was one social centre, whose owners and whose guests made it a second home for the visitor, and a most instructive school for the study of Irish life and character. Immemorially belonging to successive generations of Gregorys, of official rank and great local consideration, Coole Park, near Gort, then had as its master Trollope's old Harrow schoolfellow, Sir William Gregory. . . In his little park, full of retainers who would have risen as one man to repel any invasion of his ancestral roof, William Gregory lived a patriarchal life simple enough in its ordinary course, but fringed with some of the circumstances proper to a stock rooted in the soil from mythical times. . . The master of Coole Park shared with his visitor most of his literary, political and especially classical tastes which had survived the bodily ill-usage of Harrow and Winchester . . Gregory and Trollope had both kept up a trifle of their Greek, as well as a little more of their Latin. They could cap each other's quotations from Virgil or Horace, or the more familiar passages of less known authors. . . To quote Charles Lever, met here among others by Trollope, the Coole Park hosts set a noble example to the whole countryside in not letting the gaieties of their well-appointed roof be interfered with by irregularly paid rents.

It is also worth reading Lady Gregory's own short book, *Coole*, complete with a plan of the house and an inventory of some of the rooms. And, of course, there are Yeats's own better-known poems which do explicitly mention Coole in the titles.

Overall, the picture we might be tempted to conjure up would fit in well with T. R. Henn's evocative recall of the 'Big House' of his own youth:

> Everywhere the Big House, with its estates surrounding it, was a centre of hospitality, of county life and society, apt

> to breed a passionate attachment . . The great demesnes had their tenantry, proud, idle, careless, kindly, with a richness of speech and folk-lore that Lady Gregory had been the first to record.

Faced with such an accumulation of encomia, it would surely be a dastardly hard-hearted person who would respond to Yeats's poem with the wish that such a house should, after all, be destroyed.

Yet a few traces of an alternative picture do intrude occasionally. Elizabeth Coxhead herself remarks, of the early married life of Sir William and Lady Gregory:

> Sir William continued to gratify what he calls his insatiable appetite for travelling. Three times during his marriage he returned as visitor to his beloved Ceylon, on the second occasion taking Augusta with him, and giving her a winter in India first. Other winters were spent in Egypt; spring in Spain or Italy, and then on to the Layards [in Venice]. He had, of course, no intention of burying himself at Coole; it was a country house for a few weeks of shooting in the late summer and early autumn.

Though presumably its 'irregularly paid rents' helped to pay for this insatiable appetite. That this place of passion and precision, of immemorial hospitality and cultured conversation, can be so casually relegated to the status of an occasional shooting lodge might rather surprise a reader of Yeats's poem.

A passing remark in an article by a respected historian of the Anglo-Irish might also give us pause:

> It would be hard to find two more reactionary landlords in the province of Connaught at the height of the land war than Lady Gregory of Coole and Edward Martyn of Tullyra.

Professor Curtis unfortunately offers no evidence for this almost parenthetical judgement, and we might, of course, prefer to rely instead on the general picture of warm landlord-tenant relations suggested in Lady Gregory's own journal and autobiography:

> *May 1905*: . . All well with the tenants, a very nice letter from Father Fahey. He says, 'through your great kindness we have the old kindly relations preserved. I can assure you of the gratitude of the tenantry and of mine. '
>
> *[1903?]* The new Land Bill was going through the House of Commons and I write: . . It is necessary that as democracy gains power, our power ['we landowners'] should go; and God knows many of our ancestors and forerunners have eaten sour grapes and we must not repine if our teeth are set on edge. I would like to leave a good memory and not a ''monument of champagne bottles', and with all that, I hope to save the home, the house and woods at least for Robert.

Professort Curtis's remark and Lady Gregory's own distinction between Coole Park as landlord's estate and as 'the home' may remind us that Coole Park remained a working estate even after Sir William sold off two-thirds of it. We might also remind ourselves that fifteen of those tenants took Lady Gregory to court in 1909. And though Sir William on his death in 1892 did not leave Coole Park to Lady Gregory but to their son Robert, nevertheless she was to receive from Sir William's estate an income of £800 a year for life.

£800 a year

Is this a 'relevant historical fact'? Does it give us something definite and objective to hold onto? Perhaps we should try to calculate the value today of 800 pounds sterling in 1892. I am told, by colleagues in other disciplines, that there are several ways to do this.

I could, for example, consult the offical Price Index, which in 1985 (when I first asked this question) stood at 359, with a base-line of 100 in 1974, and a figure of 11.1 for 1914. For the period from 1890 to 1914 I had to consult another index and multiply my figures for 1914 by 1.15. Trusting these calculations I arrived, in 1985, at around £29,754 a year.

But there is another respectable way to estimate the value in 'real' terms. A Dublin labourer was, according to one source, earning an average of 10 shillings a week in 1900. On 800 pounds a year Lady Gregory would have been in receipt of 15 pounds and 38 pence a week; so I could multiply the average labourer's wage in 1985 by 31 or so to get the equivalent of what her weekly income would have bought: at 100 pounds a week in 1985 that would give 3,000 pounds a week or over 150,000 pounds a year.

If the male manufacturing wage in 1985 were closer to 200 pounds a week, as some claim, thirty times that would give 6,000 pounds a week or something over 300,000 pounds a year as a 'real' equivalent, for 1985 values, of Lady Gregory's income in the 1890s.

However, another source gives 18 shillings a week as the average wage in 1909; another cites the average male manufacturing weekly wage in the UK in 1900 as 1.40 pounds.

And we would have, on any of these calculations, to make allowance for different values in Irish and English money incomes in the 1890s, the effects of changes in rates of income tax and other taxes. Nor do I know whether Lady Gregory in fact continued to receive 800 pounds, or more, or less, as the rents were reduced, or land-values fluctuated, or whether the estate stopped paying for her annuity. Any reader with the requisite skills and knowledge is invited to work out an equivalent for themselves, and to try to update the figures for whatever year seems relevant 'now'. But I, at least, have long been content to abandon any hope of an objective measure of her income.

Yet the problem is not irrelevant. I would suggest, with reasonable confidence, that our reaction to Lady Gregory's well-known hospitality and generosity to Irish writers, and the considerable charity work detailed in her autobiography, would in fact be quite significantly modified depending on whether we thought of her as having an income in 1985 terms of, say, £30,000 a year, or £150,000 or even £300,000 per year. Since the overall Retail Price Index more or less doubled between 1985 and, say, 2005 (one recent 'now') perhaps we could even award her an annual income of over half a million pounds. And if—*if*—Lady Gregory's income was mainly derived from those 'irregularly paid rents' of tenants at Coole Park, our attitude to Coole, and thus (surely?) to this poem, might be correspondingly modified.

If, however, money income is difficult to calculate, we could look at some other contemporary comparisons instead, casting our net a little wider than simply income.

For example, we might compare the quarter-acre limit specifed for families in the 1847 Gregory Clause with the size of Augusta Persse's own garden at Roxborough when she was a child: three acres. Or the overall size of the Persse estate itelf, some 6,000 acres. Even Sir William's income at that time, around 7,000 pounds a year, rather pales by comparison with the 3,000 pounds *a month* spent by the Lord Lieutenant of Ireland on entertaining during the Dublin 'season' of 1847 — at the height of the Famine. Or we might compare the budget of the Gort workhouse, near Coole Park, where one pound (£1) was considered quite sufficient, during the Famine years, to feed a pauper for thirty-four (34) weeks, with the 'gratification' of three pounds a head offered to Dublin freemen in Sir William's parliamentary election. Or we might juxtapose, say, some different accounts of dining arrangements: from an official report on Dublin tenements in 1909, and from Lady Gregory's autobiography, concerning a holiday in Venice that same year:

— a van driver, with mother-in-law and three children, in constant employment at 15/- a week, paying 2/6d rent, and having tea, bread and butter for breakfast, with cheap American bacon and cabbage, or occasionally herrings, for dinner, and tea and bread for evening meal or supper.

— a coal porter with wife and four childen, irregularly employed at 18/- a week, paying 2/6d rent, with bread, butter and tea for breakfast, bacon and cabbage, and sometimes fish, for dinner, and bread, butter and tea for the third and last meal of the day.

— a labourer with wife and four children, in constant work in summer and irregular work in winter, at 16/- a week, paying 1/6d rent, having tea and bread, and occasionally butter, for breakfast, fish for dinner and meat on Sundays with oatmeal porridge and buttermilk for supper.

— another labourer with wife and five children, in very irregular work at 14/- a week, paying 1/6d rent and having bread, butter and milk for all three meals, except that on Sunday there was bacon for dinner.

On the other hand:

In May 1909 I had a holiday and wrote to Yeats from Ca Capello, Venice, Lady Layard's house, 'I am in my old stateroom, at the corner of the water floor, looking through four ivy trellised windows at the sunlight on the water, and only hearing the splash of cars and a gondolier singing. The room is full of beautiful furniture, and when I came in last night, at midnight, from the long dusty journey and found an Italian housemaid who has welcomed me for twenty-five years, on the steps to kiss my hand, and other servants bringing Chianti in a flask and soup in a silver bowl, it felt like fairyland!'

> Yesterday . . as Lady L. and I came out from church, there was a sailor on the landing with a note from the Royal Yacht which had arrived, asking if the Queen, the Empress of Russia, Princess Victoria, a party of twelve altogether, might come to lunch at 1.00 o'clock. Lady L. said, 'Impossible'. I said, 'Possible.' She said, '2.00 o'clock.' I said '1.30', and so it was. We came strraight back and rushed to the kitchen, and the cook wasn't fussy and said it would be all right. At 1.30 they arrived, the Queen looking younger than when I had seen her a year or two ago . . A Russian Prince (attending the Empress) was next me at lunch, and the Queen next him, and she talked to him in French about the noises of Naples and the quiet of Venice. Then, when eating some, she stooped across and said, 'What lovely peas!' and she admired the wild strawberries . . Then after smoking and coffee, more curtseys and handshakes and they left. The Queen and Empress are inseparable and the time the Empress is to leave is kept a secret, as there are said to be anarchists about looking for her.

It would be fairly easy to continue offering fragments of quotations, snippets of data, to bring a variety of perspectives upon Lady Gregory's income and life-style. But there is a real difficulty in bringing any of this into relation with the poem. Undoubtedly, our reaction to Lady Gregory and to Coole Park might be influenced by trying to hold simultaneously in mind the conditions in Dublin tenements and her vacation in Venice.

But any such juxtaposition or comparison cannot directly help us to answer the question actually posed by 'Upon a House', since insofar as the question concerns 'this house', trying to trace a real connection between that house, taken in isolation, and slum conditions in Dublin would not be easy. To do that, we would have to change the question into a different though related one, and ask instead whether the abolition of a whole class of Anglo-Irish gentry, or of wealthy landowners in general, 'we landlords' or all people "living on unearned income', would have benefitted Dublin slum-dwellers. But that, we have to acknowledge, is not the question posed, nor the framework offered.

For the connection postulated in the poem is one between 'this house' and "'the world', and that relation—the more we probe it—is an awkward one. For it would be hard not to concede, if we take the world as our frame of reference, that on that scale of comparison, my own income and my own house, and probably the income and houses of most of my likely readers, would be aligned more with the Lady Gregory end of the global scale. It would not be difficult, after all, to choose some juxtapositioning of data concerning my own meals and the diet available in drought-stricken Sudan, or to compare the solidity and inflated value of of my own semi-detached three-storey house with the cardboard boxes of those who live along the railway tracks of Guatemala City. I could come nearer home, remembering the folded newspapers and sleeping bags under Hungerford Bridge across the Thames.

It is in fact the global comparison that the poem suggests, and though I hasten to point out that I have never dined with an Empress (though I have holidayed in Venice) and that my house is heavily mortgaged (but Lady Gregory did not own Coole either), I can recognise that from several perspectives the poem's question applies also to my own situation. And, certainly, if I ask the question about this house, my own (or yours?) there would be a definite reluctance to equate that question simply and entirely with a question about the role and function of a class, or what my monthly mortgage repayments might mean for starving children in Ethiopia. Nor would I necessarily feel any very pressing responsibility for the role in world finance of my mortgage company, if it were argued that my monthly repayments are contributions to international capitalism and do therefore link me to exploitative investments across the globe.

I am aware of all these factors, yet faced with a question about *this* house (mine) I would immediately become aware of, shall we say, 'methodological' difficulties in making too immediate a connection with exploitative global relations.

It may seem that I am pressing too hard or inappropriately on a particular formulation in Yeats's poem. But it is precisely by taking the question of this poem as literally as possible, by retarding its poetic effect, that I am seeking to explore the full dimensions of what it might mean for us to read it. Posing a version of the poem's question now, to myself, is one way of highlighting the problem of specificity involved in answering the question about this house—not other houses or a class of houses, but Coole Park in 1909. But, after all, if the question only concerns Coole Park, we have no answer to give: the house was demolished in 1941.

passion and precision

We should perhaps backtrack a little here. To say that Jeffares is 'obviously' justified in naming 'this house' as Coole Park seems both correct and inadequate. The fact remains that Yeats did not so name the house of his poem, and the poem can work upon us even if we know nothing or little about the actual Coole Park. But the poem clearly defines 'this house' as a certain kind of house, one where 'passion and precision have been one'. Insofar as this is a matter of picturing the actual Coole Park we might well demur. Yeats himself must have been well aware that such phrases as 'time out of mind' did not really apply to Coole Park. Even if T.H.S. Escott could casually and inaccurately write of the house as "immemorially belonging to generations of Gregorys", Yeats can hardly have forgotten that the house was actually bought by Robert Gregory only in 1768, a mere fifty years before Sir William himself was born, and that Coole had been for many years only an occasional shooting lodge.

Yeats must also have been aware that any special status he was suggesting for Coole Park applied to it only insofar as it was *not* representative of a whole class of country estates. Even Roxborough, Lady Gregory's own family home, would hardly have fitted the picture conjured up for us, if we accept Coxhead's account:

> Roxborough was a totally unbookish house. There was no library, and no encouragement for the exchanging of ideas. 'As a child our drawing room evenings were not for conversation,' she says in the preface to *The Kiltartan Poetry Book*, 'the elders of the family keeping what little talk there was between piano-playing and newspapers to themselves; and I the youngest girl, at the fireless side of the round table, was glad enough to be seen and not heard, to win what glimpse of literature I could from the few books that lay there.' They were chiefly ornamental books; the nearest thing to a 'glimpse of literature' was Moore's *Lalla Rookh*; though elsewhere she speaks of a few old epics and histories, and it was perhaps at Roxborough that she got her love for Malory. Generally, however, she was starved of books, and reduced to borrowing from the village schoolmaster, whose stock cannot have been extensive either.

Certainly, insofar as Roxborough was more typical of the gentry houses and their culture, any claims about Coole Park could hardly be used as a justification for attributing the same qualities to a whole class of houses. Yet, conversely, Yeats must also have recognised that without the existence of that whole class, without at least the intricate relations of an inter-marrying caste, Coole Park would not have been possible. It required for its actual conditions of existence a network of other 'Big Houses' and the class-power and highly unequal distribution of land and wealth which sustained them.

Are we, then, to regard 'Upon a House' as simply a form of tactical intervention, as trying to make, at least on its first publication in December 1910, an essentially political plea for some kind of special treatment for Coole Park, some claim that it be treated as an exception, that some provision be made for *this* house, and no other, to exempt it from the effects of the judicial rent review? Or is Yeats driven, however willingly or hypocritically, to argue an implicit case for the preservation also of houses like Roxborough? And is that case, as applied to Coole Park itself, basically a spurious one anyway: that a 150-year-old shooting lodge was not, after all, a house 'where passion and precision have been one / Time out of mind"? It would be possible to interpret Yeats's action in publishing the poem in a number of ways; but that is not the same as actually reading the poem.

If we spiral back to what might be involved in our present response to the poem, these questions have to be taken into account, but also more complicated processes and problems than trying to decide what Yeats had in mind in 1909, 1910 or later.

Undoubtedly, for a start, many readers of the poem will also have in their own minds, as they read, memories of other later poems by Yeats which are explicitly about Coole. The phrases and lines in 'Upon a House' —'lidless eye that loves the sun', ''sweet laughing eagle thoughts', etc.— may in themselves not move us very powerfully at all, but even if we don't respond to those images positively, or to the images from Blake that underpin them, we might have our reactions to this poem modified and reinforced by memories of other lines:

Sound of a stick upon the floor, a sound
From somebody that toils from chair to chair;
Beloved books that famous hands have bound,
Old marble heads, old pictures everywhere;
Great rooms where travelled men and children found
Content or joy; a last inheritor
Where none has reigned that lacked a name and fame
Or out of folly into folly came.

'Coole Park, 1929'

I meditate upon a swallow's flight,
Upon an agèd woman and her house,
A sycamore and lime-tree lost in night
Although that western cloud is luminous,
Great works constructed there in nature's spite
For scholars and for poets after us,
Thoughts long knitted into a single thought,
A dance-like glory that those walls begot.

'Coole Park and Ballylee, 1931'

Those later lines may be rhetorically and emotionally more effective for particular readers than 'Upon a House'. But though they might, as they shadow this poem, reinforce an acceptance that Coole Park was somehow 'special', they provide us with no answer to the actual question of the poem.

'Coole Park, 1929' does spell out a definite reaction to one possibility for the house, in anticipation:

Here, traveller, scholar, poet, take your stand
When all those rooms and passages are gone,
When nettles wave upon a shapeless mound
And saplings root among the broken stone,
And dedicate—eyes bent upon the ground,
Back turned upon the brightnes of the sun
And all the sensuality of the shade—
A moment's memory to that laurelled head.

But this is not, after all, what is proposed for us in 'Upon a House'.It is actually quite difficult to know what, in practice, even in 1909 or 1910, a specific answer could have been. Beneath the 'rhetorical questions' is a more difficult question and problem, one to which it would be inadequate to reply merely by a bowed head and a moment's memory.

upon other houses

What actually happens for me is that—given that I never knew Coole Park anyway—I find myself thinking, almost necessarily it seems, of other houses which have indeed operated for me as special, exceptional places. I respond to the *kind* of house Coole Park is represented as being by calling upon my own experience of that 'kind' of house.

In particular, I think of one house: Kettle's Yard, in Cambridge. Not that Kettle's Yard is at all similar to Coole in its architecture, or history, or several other respects; but it does act as a my image of what Yeats's poem invites me to admire in Coole Park.

Those who don't know Kettle's Yard can get some sense of it from a book of detailed photographs and commentary published in 1984, *A Way of Life* (Cambridge University Press), and from some of the comments quoted in the book:

> — Its colour is a natural one; scrubbed wood, stone pottery, brick floors, biscuit, with a kind of powdery white that finds its way off the walls in concealed daylight, and quietly keeps everything fresh, ascetic, clear.

> — The house is so folded in on itself that, once indoors, only when you listen are you aware of the surrounding heavy traffic . . Where light sources are not concealed, windows are full of plants, china and glass, so that daylight arrives in the rooms through green leaves or reflected and refracted off a variety of hard surfaces. It is central to the philosophy of Kettle's Yard that a room is already furnished by the light that comes into it.

Jim Ede, whose home Kettle's Yard was, expresses something of that 'philosophy' in talking about the origins of the house:

> It was while we were still abroad in 1954 that I found myself dreaming of the idea of somehow creating a living place where works of art would be enjoyed, inherent to the domestic setting, where young people could be at home unhampered by the greater austerity of the museum or public art gallery, and where an informality might infuse an underlying formality. I wanted, in a modest way, to use the inspiration I had had from beautiful interiors, houses of leisured elegance; and to combine it with the joy I had felt in individual works seen in museums, and with the all embracing delight I had experienced in nature; in stones, in flowers, in people. . . But how could this be managed without money?

In the end, Jim Ede found and converted 'four tiny condemned slum dwellings' just near a busy traffic intersection in a congested part of Cambridge. Each cottage, before their combination into one house, was only about ten feet square, but by adding bay windows, by the use of white walls, scattered rugs, bare floorboards, and an extraordinarily sensitive placing of furniture, Ede created a sense of marvellous light and space. Even without the paintings, sculptures and other works which Ede had acquired over the years, the house would have been a place of peace and stillness. But, in addition, one small bedroom—to take a manageable example—contained in its seven feet by nine feet a work by Henry Moore, two by Alfred Wallis, a John Blackburn, a Gaudier-Brzeska, a David Jones watercolour, and seven works by Ben Nicholson. In all, there were about 400 works of art in this still smallish house. Yet the collection was not built upon great personal wealth, but largely upon friendships and gifts:

> I turned out to be one of Ben Nicholson's very few admirers at that time, and after he had tried to sell a painting for a year or so he would tell me that I could have it for the price of the canvas and frame, usually one to three pounds. I could not always manage it, for my salary

> was under 250 pounds a year; not much to maintain a family in London. [in the 1930s]
>
> I think it was in 1926 I first began to get paintings by Alfred Wallis. They would come by post, perhaps 60 at a time, and the price fixed at 1/-, 2/-, 3/- according to size. I once got twenty but usually could not afford so many.
>
> Miro gave me a small painting one sunny morning as we drank coffee in a Paris street. . . Chagall offered me anything in his studio for 60 pounds, and some of his finest paintings were there. A small Rouault or one by Rousseau was probably 25 pounds.

Even so, the monetary value of the whole of Kettle's Yard must now be incalculable.

Immediately next door to Jim Ede's converted cottages is a small row of houses, designed and built by the local council for old age pensioners. It was perfectly apparent, of course, that these two types of home were separated by a lot more than a few yards. Yet if any proposal had been made, say, to demolish Kettle's Yard, sell off and disperse the collection and use the cash-value of those Gaudier-Brzeskas and Ben Nicholsons to extend the housing available for old age pensioners in Cambridge, I am aware that I would have been, in practice, opposed. Had the proposal ever been made to spend several millions of council money (or university money) to enable those pensioners to convert their houses also into something approaching Kettle's Yard, that might have been a more interesting proposition.

For one effect of Kettle's Yard was to stimulate a desire for everyone to have, if not that particular way of life, according to that particular aesthetic conception of environment and taste, at least something in the same fundamental spirit. I can therefore read Yeats's comment in his Journal, about this poem, with some degree of recognition and endorsment:

> One feels that when all must make their living they will live not for life's sake but for the work's and all be the poorer . . This house has enriched my soul out of measure because here life moves within restraint through gracious forms. Here there has been no compelled labour, no poverty-thwarted impulse.

Yet even with a sense of what a Kettle's Yard might mean —and part of the point of this excursus is to suggest that each reader of the poem might have similar experiences to draw upon—and though I do have a sharper sense of the force of the poem's questions, I know nevertheless that my endorsement of Yeats's implicit case is by no means total.

For at the same time as Kettle's Yard mingles in my mind with Coole Park, I find myself also thinking of another kind of house, one which offers — in the instance I shall use— a more direct comparison with Coole. Yeats's poem, 'In Memory of Eva Gore-Booth and Con Markiewicz' begins:

> The light of evening, Lissadell,
> Great windows open to the south,
> Two girls in silk kimonos, both
> Beautiful, one a gazelle.

Readers of Yeats's work will be more or less familiar with that image of Lissadell, the Gore-Booths' grey granite house overlooking Sligo Bay, designed by Francis Godwin in 1832 and built in 1837-9. Yeats recorded his own impression of it in a letter to his sister, after his first visit there, in 1894:

> Lissadell is an exceedingly impressive house inside with a great sitting room as high as a church and all things in good taste . . But outside it is grey, square and bare yet set amid delightful grounds.

It would certainly be worth investigating the local role played by the various Gore-Booths at Lissadell: the sisters' grandfather, Sir Robert, who annexed 800 acres by wholesale evictions in 1834, but also initiated the reclaiming of hundreds of acres of otherwise unuseable land from the sea's encroachment, pioneered the planting of oysters and the efficient harvesting of seaweed; their father, Sir Henry, who, during the 1879-80 famine reduced the rents by 40% but felt he could not directly break the provisions (still obtaining) of the Gregory Clause, so promised that he would take personal responsibility for all the cottages of those who left them to enter the workhouse for temporary relief; their brother, Sir Josslyn, who applied scientific experimentation to improving local livestock, potatoes, fruit and bulbs, and in 1895 organised the first cooperative creamery in Sligo. None of this, as it happens, gets into Yeats' poem about Lissadell.

But nor does the Gore-Booth house I want here to instance. Yeats never wrote a poem entitled 'Surrey House' but perhaps he should have. It was the Dublin home of Constance Gore-Booth, after her marriage to Count Casimir Markiewicz, and I want here to bring it into comparison with Coole Park.

Surrey House, on the Leinster Road in the suburb of Rathmines, to which the Markiewicz family moved in 1911, is described by Con's biographer, Jacqueline Van Voris:

> Surrey House became synonymous with hospitality and insurrection. It was always open to Fianna boys, any of Madame's republican or labour friends, visiting journalists, plotters of revolution and convalescents from the rigours of prison. She rolled up the rugs to simplify house cleaning, and there was always bread and tea and talk. There was a small platen model printing press on which all kinds of seditious posters, slogans and handbills were printed to be distributed round town. . . as the date for the 1916 Rising neared, one French journalist reported that the salon of Madame Markiewicz was not a salon, it was an army headquarters.

> It was from Surrey House that the trade union leader Jim Larkin set out for his brief, banned appearance in O'Connell Street, which sparked off Bloody Sunday in 1913. It was to Surrey House that the socialist organiser James Connolly was taken to recover from his prison hunger strike in the same year, and it was at Surrey House that he made his reappearance after the crucial meeting with the Irish Republican Brotherhood to set the date of the Easter Rising. And after the Rising it was inevitable that Surrey House, not for the first time, should have been raided and sacked by police and soldiers. Surrey House was the base from which Con Markiewicz established her formidable involvement in so many organisations—the Fianna scouts, Sinn Fein, the Citizen Army, the women's movements—which was to lead her to her role in the rising, her reprieved death sentence, and her Cabinet post as Minister for Labour in the first Dail. It was also, and simultaneously, the base from which Count Markiewicz organised art exhibitions and the Independent Theatre Company.

Placing images of Kettle's Yard and Surrey House in interaction with that of Coole Park may be idiosyncratic, in terms of my individual choices for comparison. Yet it seems to me an almost inescapable part of the process of responding to this poem. T. S. Eliot's advice on reading poems—'we can only criticise according to standards, in comparison to other works of art'—has a certain application here. If I am genuinely to answer the question of this poem, I find I have to do so primarily by a kind of judgement and comparison between particulars.

mere ideology?

There may seem, at first, a simpler mode of response and judgement available, one which would analyse the poem's 'ideological' conflations and insist instead on a distinction between different aspects and functions of what Coole Park was, to some of which one might respond positively, to others negatively. One useful way of analysing a statement as 'ideological' is to locate a key term which operates with a systematic ambiguity, hinging and conflating two very different senses.

Ernst Gellner has argued that an expression such as 'your betters' is such an ideological conflation, and Denys Turner has applied his suggestion to a sentence from George Eliot's novel, *Felix Holt*, in which Felix's widowed mother appeals to the rich landowner Harold Transome:

> . . and I know as you're told . . not to rail at your betters if they be the devil himself.

'Your betters' here both defines a certain social class as morally 'better' and recognises that the devil himself—hardly a moral exemplar—could belong to that same 'better' class, socially defined. Mrs Holt's total sentence discloses the systematic but effective ambiguity which sustains the term 'your betters' in its ideological role.

We could similarly analyse the terms 'house' and 'gifts' in Yeats's poem. 'House' designates in one sense the building, Coole Park, yet a building as such is not characterised by qualities of 'passion and precision"; "house' stands simultaneously for a way of life, or family tradition, and it is that which the poem praises; yet in asking the question, literally, of the house becoming 'too ruinous' to sustain that tradition, the poem moves across an ideological conflation, a question-begging ambiguity. Even more so, the term 'gifts' hovers between a sense we might interpret in financial and power terms (the money that bought a Parliamentary seat, the cozy relation to power that could simply request a governorship), and a quite different sense, that of talent or capacities, 'natural' gifts. Clearly, these two senses are not necessarily united in any particular case, though the poem implicitly conflates them.

We could move from such analyses to a rejection of any such conflations and respond that we have, for example, no objection to the continued physical existence of a rather drab example of 18th century architecture but object strongly to the perpetuation of the gentry class, or the specific family that had resided there. Alternatively, we might be prepared to see the house itself demolished, provided the tradition of culture associated with it was otherwise maintained. We could also reject the very notion of some people having a 'natural gift' to govern others, while not even objecting to Sir William spending, say, 800 pounds on a race horse or on decorating the drawing room.

Some readers may have made this kind of distinction almost spontaneously and immediately in their first response to the poem. But I want to suggest that the poem's actual question does not so easily allow us to operate that distinction. The question focuses on *this* house and it was undeniably the case that without the support of Lady Gregory, made possible by the income and history of Coole Park, the particular cultural achievements of Yeats and others would not have occurred in the way that they did. We might argue that whatever the cultural achievements made possible by Coole, it was in some sense preferable that Coole should not have existed or should rapidly have ceased to exist. We might prefer that such achievements had been possible in some other way. In either case, we are postulating a position similar to that explored earlier: judging that the history of the world could or should have been different. And it is not yet clear what kind of judgement is involved in that argument.

At this point, the comparison with Surrey House assumes part of its relevance, since we know, from the case of Surrey House, that a very similar economic basis *could* indeed enable other possibilities, even in 1909. And the example of Kettle's Yard gives us a specific instance of a form of cultural achievement which did not rest upon that kind of basis at all. But thinking about these issues in terms of specific instances recognises that the question posed in the poem is a specific question—which could also apply to Surrey House and to Kettle's Yard. Of these houses too, it would make sense to ask how the world would be luckier if they were not to exist, and in all three cases it could be argued that 'mean roof trees' might indeed be the better for their fall.

But since the function of maintaining cultural achievement is not dissociable in practice from the actual instantiation of that function in some material location and particularity, we can never simply opt for the approved-of function in the abstract. We have, quite concretely, to decide whether *this* house is to be maintained or destroyed, whether the ''house' in question is an 18th century mansion or a university, an art gallery or a theatre. Thus, what from one angle can seem an ideological conflation, from another is the political problem actually posed by the poem. The poem refuses the distinctions, even flaunts the conflations, and asks a genuinely political question, one of decisions, priorities and strategy: would you, in 1909, destroy this house or allow it to be destroyed? It is part of the political character of the question that we can recognise an 'ideological' conflation at work in its formulation. But could a political question ever be formulated without such conflation?

Yet on what basis would we then answer the question and make the decision? An analytical distinction is not a decision, though it may be a necessary stage in making one. But if we can't simply offer the distinction as our decision, on what basis do we decide? And, of course, if we refuse that question, decline to make—even hypothetically—that decision, are we not again retreating from even attempting to exercise 'the gifts that govern men', opting instead for the easier activity, that of 'reading literature' or 'writing criticism', regarded as a matter of words and only words?

If so, we can at least think about one of the more surprising words in the poem.

moral luck

The poem begins: 'how should the world be luckier . .?' 'Luckier' is a somewhat odd choice of word—yet it was, as is clear from the draft, a deliberate choice, preferred to the 'better' which appears in both the prose version in the Journals and in the first verse draft. The same term recurs in

'How should their luck run high enough to reach . .?' We could try to gloss the term 'luck' according to various dictionary definitions, or Yeats' own usage elsewhere, and we could probably analyse a certain systematic ideological ambiguity or conflation in how it operates within the poem, hovering between a sense of determined fate and of random happenstance, between a sense of 'fortunate' and a sense of mere 'lot''. I don't, however, want to to offer so much an interpretation of the word as a way of analysing it which makes clearer the kind of question posed by the poem.

The philosopher Bernard Williams has written an intriguing essay entitled 'Moral Luck', in which he considers and argues against the position which holds that 'at the ultimate and most important level, it cannot be a matter of luck whether [an agent] was justified in doing what he did. ' I will try to compress Williams' argument into a few quotations from his essay and then consider Yeats' poem in the light of his argument. Williams writes:

> Let us take first an outline example of the creative artist who turns away from definite and pressing human claims on him in order to live a life in which, as he supposes, he can pursue his art. Without feeling that we are limited by any historical facts, let us call him Gauguin.
>
> . . Let us take a Gauguin who is concerned about these claims and what is involved in their being neglected (we may suppose this to be grim), and that he nevertheless, in the face of that, opts for that other life. . . it is as a life which will enable him really to be a painter that he opts for it.
>
> . . Whether he will succeed cannot, in the nature of the case, be forseen. We are not dealing here with the removal of an external obstacle to something which, once that is removed, will fairly predictably go through. Gauguin, in our story, is putting a great deal on a possibility which has not unequivocally declared itself. I want to explore and uphold the claim that in such a situation the only thing

that will justify his choice will be success itself. If he fails . . then he did the wrong thing not just in the sense in which that platitudinously follows, but in the sense that having done the wrong thing in those circumstances he has no basis for the thought that he was justified in acting as he did. If he succeeds, he does have a basis for that thought.

. . If Gauguin sustains some injury on the way to Tahiti which prevents him ever painting again, that certainly means that his decision (supposing it now to be irreversible) was for nothing, and indeed there is nothing in the outcome to set against the other people's loss. But that train of events does not provoke the thought . . that after all he was wrong and unjustified. . . What would prove him wrong in his project would not just be that it failed, but that he failed.

. . the obvious fact [is] that what one does and the sort of life one leads conditions one's later desires and judgments. The standpoint of that retrospective judge who will be my later self will be the product of my earlier choices.

. . The perspective of deliberative choice on one's life is constitutively from here. Correspondingly, the perspective of assessment with greater knowledge is necessarily from there, and not only can I not guarantee how factually it will then be, but I cannot ultimately guarantee from what standpoint of assessment my major and and most fundamental regrets will be.

. . In these cases the project in the interests of which the decision is made is one with which the agent is identified in such a way that if it succeeds, his standpoint of assessment will be from a life which then derives an important part of its significance for him from that very fact; if he fails, it can, necessarily, have no such significance in his life. If he succeeds, it cannot be that while welcoming the outcome he more basically regrets the decision. If he fails, his standpoint will be of one for whom the ground project of the decision has proved worthless, and this (under the simplifying assumption that other adequate projects are not generated in the process) must leave him with the most basic regrets. So if he fails, his most basic regrets will attach to his decision, and if he succeeds, they cannot. That is the sense in which his decision can be justified, for him, by success.

Williams' argument, thus compressed, suggests a way of considering the question of Yeats' poem. If we think of that poem as from the point of view of Yeats in 1909, we could argue that the question, as posed for him, involves a moral luck issue. It is not primarily in terms of any alleged ancestral past of Coole Park that he would want to defend it against demolition or decay, but rather in terms of a postulate about its future and his future. Though it may be offered as part of that argument that the general history of the house makes a certain kind of future likely, what is specifically at stake for Yeats is that Coole Park does in 1909 foster, and he hopes will continue to foster in the future, his own talent, enable his own writing and that of others whom he admires.

What is clearly involved, therefore, in reading the poem is Yeats' own stature as a poet. In 1909 he was 44. In 1908 he had published his first *Collected Works*, in eight volumes. He was clearly conceiving of himself as, at least potentially, a 'major' poet. But if that potential was, in Yeats's eyes to some extent dependent upon the continued support of Coole Park both financially and as a writing retreat then, though he can recognise that a cost for others might be involved (the syntax of 'though' mean roof-trees 'were' the sturdier allows an ambiguity), he would still want to opt for the maintenance of those conditions which, in enabling his own future achievement, would also permit him retrospectively to justify that admitted cost.

To apply the question in this way to Yeats's own case is not, of course, to restrict it to his case. The basic gesture of the poem is to generalise that moral luck issue, though with Yeats as an unavoidable implicit instance.

But the implications of this for a reader of Yeats's poems now are complex. The reader is not, after all, either an agent or a victim of this decision but rather a later spectator, not asking about an unknown future but looking back from that future. If 'moral luck' decisions involve retrospective justification, are we now in a position to confirm or deny that justification?

If it is a matter of assessing how far Yeats succeeded in becoming a major poet, the slightly odd consequence would be that involved in our answer to the question of 'Upon a House' would be a judgement not so much, or not only, on this poem alone but also upon his whole *oeuvre*, on every poem Yeats wrote, but especially perhaps those written after 1909. Poems such as 'Coole Park 1929' and 'Coole Park & Ballylee 1931' would then not only shadow this poem as providing relevant accompanying and reinforcing images of Coole; our judgement of them as either successful or unsuccessful poems would itself enter into our response to the very question asked in 'Upon a House'—and so would our judgement of all Yeats's work. In a rather curious way, Eliot's claim, in 'What is Minor Poetry?', that a major poet is one the whole of whose work we ought to read, in order fully to appreciate any part of it, would seem to find a new and specific application.

But we should recall that though a moral luck justification may be offered by the agent from his retrospective perspective, that justification need not be acceptable to a spectator, still less to a victim of the cost involved. As spectators of the moral luck choice evoked in Yeats's poem we would still have to weigh any assessment of Yeats as a major poet, or otherwise, against our own judgement of the cost involved to others. From Yeats's point of view he might be retrospectively justified in prioritising Coole Park over mean roof-trees if in doing so he were enabled to become a major poet. On Bernard Williams's argument he could not, retrospectively, regret such a choice. But this would by no means obligate the Coole tenants to endorse that prioritisation—even if they themselves recognised the later

Yeats as having 'succeeded'. And as readers, now, of the poem and of the whole *oeuvre,* do we simply have to choose between these putative perspectives, that of Yeats and that of the tenants, or is there a third way of reading the poem, specifically from our own perspective?

responsibilities

First, however, we can pursue Yeats's own perspective further. If we, as readers, are to assess how far we consider Yeats might have succeeded in becoming a great poet, we will have to take into account more poems than 'Upon a House'—though we will return to that pivotal poem in due course.

The title of his next important volume of poems, *Responsibilities* (1914) is consonant with the notion that he was now regarding himself as having the status of a major poet.

One variation of the moral luck pattern underlies one of the central poems of the volume: 'To a Wealthy Man who promised a second subscription to the Dublin Municipal Gallery if it were proved the people wanted pictures.' The basic situation referred to in the poem is perhaps familiar: that Lady Gregory's nephew, Hugh Lane, had donated a collection of modern paintings to Dublin provided an appropriate gallery was built to house them. The city corporation refused to meet that condition (the suggested gallery would have cost around 20,000 pounds, it was claimed) and an attempt at private financing failed. The poem was written in 1912.

> You gave, but will not give again
> Until enough of Paudeen's pence
> By Biddy's halfpennies have lain
> To be 'some sort of evidence',
> Before you'll put your guineas down,
> That things it were a pride to give
> Are what the blind and ignorant town

Imagines best to make it thrive.
What cared Duke Ercole, that bid
His mummers to the market-place,
What th'onion-sellers thought or did
So that his Plautus set the pace
For the Italian comedies?

The poem itself does not make explicit that any cost to others might be involved in the proposed investment in an art gallery for Dublin; but we can recall Yeats' own admission that the money involved could indeed have been spent on improving Dublin slum housing: he said he recognised the force of the argument but despised those who offered it as an excuse for doing neither. Whatever the weight of that argument, Yeats is proposing that certain people should choose to spend money on an art gallery even if, the implicit valuation goes, the very people for whom it was intended would prefer the money be spent other-wise. The justification for doing so concerns the future:

Let paudeens play at pitch and toss,
Look up in the sun's eye and give
What the exultant heart calls good
That some new day may breed the best
Because you gave, not what they would,
But the right twigs for an eagle's nest.

That future is not, of course, guaranteed. Indeed, it might be thought that the argument is, logically, very weak indeed: why should the "paudeens' of the future have any more interest in art than those of the present? The mere fact of a gallery being there, available to be visited, can hardly guarantee that the paudeens will abandon their pitch and toss and become art lovers.

But the function of the references to Ercole, Guidobaldo and Cosimo is, I suggest, more complex than simply to provide historical examples of wealthy rulers who ignored the desires of their 'paudeens'. Yeats's particular references should remind us that at the time of those patrons 'Italy' as a single nation did not exist, yet that an important part of the self-identity of that nation finally constituted as 'Italy' in the nineteenth century was contributed by the claim that there was an 'Italian Renaissance". In one of his Journal entries Yeats remarks that Dante "invented' Italy. The underlying argument and hope of the poem can therefore be read as evoking a future in which what will matter will not simply be that poor Dubliners learn to admire Raphael but that, at some time, the very cultural identity of a newly-recreated Irish nation will rest, at least retrospectively, upon the achievements of the generations which made possible, once again, an 'Irish' culture. Art galleries to encourage and stimulate Irish art may be important in that larger process.

This is, however, rather like Gauguin's future in Bernard Williams's argument, a matter of 'moral luck'. Not only might the gallery suffer some accidental fate (shelled to pieces in 1916 perhaps) but the implicit claim that an Irish nation will be capable of, and will somehow find and create, a cultural identity rests upon a belief not only in the general possibility of establishing or maintaining a continuity between a repressed past and a revived future but also in the specific possibility of such as Yeats becoming, or making themselves into, the effective cultural inheritors and re-creators of that tradition. This poem therefore appeals, indirectly, not simply to an assessment of Yeats but to a judgement on the potential of a whole generation.

'To a Wealthy Man' revolves, therefore, upon a variation of a characteristic stance of an artistic "avant-garde', that of trying to create the taste by which they are enjoyed, and only success in that can, and then only retrospectively, justify the stature they claim for their art. Again, a matter of a certain luck. We can, however, extend this underlying parallel still further, by examining also the stance of the political vanguard party and with it several more of Yeats' crucial poems.

Easter 1916

If we consider the actions of those who organised the Easter rising in 1916 we have to recognise the large element of moral luck to which they also implicitly appealed. It was clear—certainly after the scuttling of the ship carrying German weapons and the confusing counter-manding of mobilisation orders—that the rising was almost certain to 'fail' in immediate terms, and that the cost would be very high, not just for the participants but for others too. James Connolly may have harboured the illusion that the British forces would restrict themselves to small arms and would refrain—as the army of the capitalist class—from using artillery on the private commercial buildings of central Dublin; but he was soon enlightened. The shelling and destruction of large parts of the capital was the most visible cost of that doomed military operation; the execution of the leaders was the most dramatic. That Connolly was aware in advance of the personal cost is evidenced by several accounts of his remark as the Irish Citizen Army marched out on the first morning of the rising: 'We are going out to die.'

In 1916 such costs could only be justified by a calculation about the future, and it would be easy to say that the future did, quite quickly, vindicate the moral wager taken by the 1916 insurgents. Though the reaction of most Dubliners was at best indifferent and often hostile during the rising itself, that mood changed, progressively and permanently, it seemed. By 1919 the events of 1916 were already felt to mark the new birth of the nation; the General Post Office became, in a sense, the foundation stone of a risen people.

If we look briefly here at Yeats' poem 'Easter 1916' we can indeed see that it registers a sense of that moral gamble. On September 25th 1916, which is the date Yeats appends to the poem, one could still have asked as a real question:

Was it needless death after all?
For England may keep faith
For all that is done and said.

If Home Rule could have been confirmed without the Rising, then the cost of the rising itself would have seemed morally unjustified. Yet such possible futures could not be known in 1916 and such alternative futures can only, after the event, be speculation. Yet what the poem does is not simply to register this familiar political crux. It moves, explicitly, from the position of spectatorship to a position more akin to that of agent. In the transition from

I have met them at close of day
Coming with vivid faces

to the final song

I write it out in a verse

the Yeats of the poem assumes a stance which in its own way partakes of a moral luck decision. The final movement of the poem commits the speaker to an affirmation and endorsement which, in September 1916, could only await its possible retrospective justification, from a future neither known nor inevitable.

We know their dream; enough
To know they dreamed and are dead;
And what if excess of love
Bewildered them till they died?
I write it out in a verse —
MacDonagh and MacBride
And Connolly and Pearse
Now and in time to be
Wherever green is worn,
Are changed, changed utterly:
A terrible beauty is born.

Difficult as it may 'now' be, we should recognise how strangely these lines would read today (if we were still to read them at all) if by 1920 other events had in fact overtaken the impact of 1916 and the martyrs of the rising had, in the light of quite other happenings, been seen now as only marginal and temporary in their impact upon events. In late 1916 that was still a possible future; by 1921 when the poem appeared in volume form, the final lines had already, it must have seemed, received their confirmation. But it is arguable that not only our overall response to the poem but even our judgement of it in ostensibly aesthetic terms rests upon that historical confirmation: when it was actually written it was perhaps not quite as good a poem as it has now become.

Any move from spectator to agent is however internal to the poem. In actual politics, Yeats himself remained largely a spectator of events for some time to come. Had the poem been widely disseminated in 1916 in such a way as to help crystallise and articulate a still volatile public reaction to the rising, Yeats might indeed have figured as an important agent, with all the moral responsibilities attached. The delay in the poem's effective appearance— in 1916 it was printed only in a limited edition of 25 copies—till 1920 (in *The Statesman*) and 1921 (in *Michael Robartes and the Dancer*) would have the effect of its then being read as more simply echoing, rather than enabling, the general shift in response from a relatively indifferent spectatorship to massive endorsement and then active involvement in the struggle of 'Sinn Fein' during the period 1918-21.

Yet the fact that it was 'Sinn Fein' which became the focus for the struggle after the rising raises very directly the question of what, after all, could count as 'success' for those who took part in the rising itself. As an organised party the Sinn Fein of 1916 had not in fact participated. The crucial organisers were the Irish Republican Brotherhood, operating covertly within the Volunteers, and the Irish Citizen Army, with Connolly as perhaps the really effective driving force during the final decisions and the actual fighting. If we ask what the objectives of that mixed bag of participants were, and what they would have regarded as the "success' which would retrospectively justify their actions, we encounter ambiguity and diversity. For the various participants had rather distinct long-term objectives.

The clearest and most basic distinction was between Connolly's desired future as socialist, with national independence as a step towards that goal, and those who wanted an independence defined primarily in other terms. Once Connolly's specific perspective was in large part removed by his execution, it became increasingly apparent that national independence as an objective in itself could mean many different things. Not only was there the continuing problem of how far a national independence had been achieved if "Ulster' (itself now re-defined by a new border) remained within the United Kingdom and what, precisely, independence meant in constitutional terms (the early contention over the oath of allegiance); there was, increasingly, the problem of what any "national independence' could possibly mean in the global economic conditions of the 20th century.

A sufficiently clear expression of one facet of the problem was given many years ago by James Meehan in his *The Irish Economy since 1922*:

> It was (and is) taken for granted that the justification of self-government was to provide a better life for the Irish people and it was (and is) assumed that a better life meant a better life in Ireland. But suppose it did not? Suppose that many of the Irish people decided that life abroad was preferable to anything that could be provided in Ireland?. . . . Prosperity in the United States or full employment in the United Kingdom may therefore cause emigration irrespective of conditions in Ireland itself. The volume of trade carried on by the Irish economy is comparatively large for its size. But the composition and the volume of the export trade may be largely determined, as has happened in recent years, by the policies adopted in the UK to support British agriculture. On the import side sharp changes in world prices such as occurred in 1950-51 may turn the balance of payments topsy-turvy. At any time

the economy may be affected by influences which are wholly outside the power of an Irish government to control.

Given the difficulties, more apparent every year, of defining national independence satisfactorily for all the parties involved in trying to achieve it, it can still be asked how far the 1916 rising has been successful in the terms its organisers might have endorsed. Yet there is also a sense in which (returning to one aspect of Bernard Williams's argument) the Irish people cannot regret its occurrence, since it was and is so constitutive of the very identity—whatever that is—of that 'Irish nation' today. At least, Williams's argument would apply if it were possible coherently to think of a nation or a people as the subject of regret or as an agent of history. To do so, we might have to conflate what James Connolly would have distinguished as quite different and opposed agencies, those of class.

A number of Yeats's poems register some aspects of the central divide between Connolly and his co-participants, perhaps most concisely in the abrupt bitter poem 'Parnell':

> Parnell came down the road, he said to a cheering man:
> Ireland shall get her freedom and you still break stone.

But in the poem ''Easter 1916' any differences between Markiewicz, Pearse, Connolly, MacDonagh and MacBride can be textually conflated into a single affirmation. A song and a colour ('wherever green is worn') can 'unify' in the same way that an essentially ''cultural' notion of national identity can offer a 'unified' definition, precisely because such a cultural unity and definition can remain permanently open to quite divergent contributions and interpretations, an always postponed resolution of the unanswerable question: ''what is this national culture?'

For Yeats to have aligned his poems, before 1916, explicitly with any one faction, group, party or political perspective, as was often demanded of him, would immediately have disclosed even more clearly, at least to him, how unconflatable those different positions finally were. While Yeats offered a song that all could sing and a unity of culture all could endorse, provided that 'culture' was open to their own version of it, any one group could claim him as potentially their own. 'Easter 1916' as a poem and Easter 1916 as a political moment mark the point where such conflation could, briefly, seem to be the very truth of history. Not least because the event, in becoming a failure and therefore an annual commemoration, rather than a success and therefore an actual struggle for power, became, like a poem, an utterance that could be detached from its specific context and become a reiterated event, an occasion to be quoted on every occasion.

After the events of 1916 it would not be so easy to operate a political conflation, except by appeal to Easter 1916 itself. There is always a difference between an artistic avant-garde and a political vanguard. In the art-work, ideological conflations can be sustained which would prove impossible to reconcile in any actual political practice, and while one avant-garde may oppose another, the spectator or audience can remain indifferent, or choose neither, endorse both, or wait with equanimity for a transformed dominant 'taste' to develop. A 'successful' political vanguard, on the other hand, changes at a much more drastic and inescapable level the very conditions from which subsequent political choices can be and have to be made.

The difference between Kettles Yard and Surrey House can make the point. Whatever my admiration for or sense of gratitude to Kettles Yard, I would willingly accept and even relish the prospect of several co-existing yet different versions of Kettles Yard. But I would have to choose between several versions of Surrey House. As the sharp clash between Sean O'Casey, as secretary of the Irish Citizen Army, and Con Markiewicz herself showed, it was not possible to remain a consistent member of two organisations whose political perspectives and strategies were potentially at variance. In O'Casey's (unsuccessful) insistence that Markiewicz be forced to resign from the ICA, because of her continued membership of the Irish Volunteers, one might even see—as O'Casey was subsequently to argue—a crucial moment in Irish history, a missed opportunity. Had O'Casey had his way, and kept the two organisations wholly distinct, the trajectory of the ICA might still have led it towards some form of insurrectionary attempt, while without Connolly's military leadership and drive the efforts of the IRB alone might not have led it towards a rising. It is not inconceivable, therefore, on O'Casey's analysis, that the first armed rising of the new nation could have been conducted wholly under socialist and working class auspices. It would presumably still have 'failed' but even so the history from which we would now be reviewing questions about Coole Park might be rather different.

An artistic movement, on the other hand, can more easily accommodate co-existing rivalries, if only because artistic allegiances don't have to be settled in territorial terms. Given a split, one can always open another theatre or start a new journal: each artistic groupuscule can even declare its own house its republic. But, equally, each can continue to assert its contribution to a 'larger' entity: a national culture, left sufficiently porous to allow unresolved differences. Coole Park could therefore present itself, for a time, as a focus for a certain pluralism, a base for a fairly ecumenical patronage. The almost explicit claim advanced in 'Upon a House' is indeed that such differences as those of wealth and ownership should somehow be laid aside in the implicit recognition of Coole's contribution to 'Irish' identity. There is a parallel here, of course, with the actual rising. What was intended as crucial about the rising was not to be its specific effects, which were unforseeable in any detail, but the actual affirmation of its basis precisely as 'Irish'. The point and aim of the rising was to proclaim an 'Irish' government, whatever the unrealisable policies or politics of that doomed "government' might have been.

Yeats's own position is deeply consonant with that notion. The moral gamble he took was not that of becoming a great poet, so much as becoming an 'Irish' poet. As he points out, he had refused the one privilege his trade allowed, that of being able to work wherever he chose, in Ferrara or Urbino, Paris or London. In returning annually to Coole and in working in the Abbey Theatre, Yeats had chosen to identify himself as—if such a thing existed at all—an Irish poet. The various splits and riots, disagreements and boycotts, that punctuated the work of the Abbey insistently demonstrated that even a 'cultural' version of 'Irish unity' was beyond reach, just as the real economic basis of Coole Park demonstrated the divisions that under-pinned and under-mined such claims of unity.

Yeats could finally only transcend those real and sharp differences and actual conflicts of interest by a bold move, by a transposing of the issue onto a global plane, where such local difficulties could be lost from view: how should the *world* be luckier. . .? And in one sense he could claim to be correct. Just as the Irish 'government' could only effectively be the Irish government if it was globally recognised as such, so Yeats could only affirm the identity of being a great Irish poet if he was recognised outside Ireland as a 'great' poet in the first place. His greatness is linked with his Irishness, in a curious parallel to diplomatic recognition. In being awarded the Nobel Prize for Literature Yeats ensured that the new nation did indeed have a culture recognised as Irish.

In treating Yeats, who had spent most of his life living in England, who wrote in English, and who shared few of his fellow countrymen's beliefs or conditions of existence, as an 'Irish' poet, does one thereby accept implicitly a notion of 'Irishness' as transcending or taking priority over other descriptions and over the always substantial differences between Yeats and other 'Irish' figures? In doing so, would we even in effect be endorsing the relegation of the inhabitants of the 'mean roof trees' to a subordinate position within that notion of 'Irishness'—which, after all, is what many bourgeois theories of nationality in practice do. The interests of the 'nation' are elided into the interests of those who already have quite other identities and priorities.

There is an intriguing comparison here between Yeats and Joyce. Yeats was quite confident of his being an artist; the difficulty was in aligning himself as 'Irish'. Joyce was under no illusion that he was Irish, but a great deal of his work can be seen as negotiating the problem of what it means to become an artist—and in that perspective 'Irishness' might rather be seen as an obstacle than as a goal, an identity to be jettisoned rather than one to be constructed. Both positions can again be seen as variants of a moral luck decison. Joyce's exile, after all, has some direct affinities with Gauguin's, though Trieste is hardly Tahiti. Just as in 1916 the participants could not have known in advance what would count as an 'Irish' identity, polity and nation, so an artist cannot know in advance what specific poems will eventually constitute his or her status as artist, still less as 'national' artist. Yeats's own formulation of the gamble is clear enough:

> I have not asked my fellow workers what they mean by the words National Literature, but though I have no great love for definitions, I would define it in some such way as this: It is the work of writers who are moulded by influences that are moulding their country, and who write out of so deep a life that they are accepted there in the end. [*Samhain*, 1904]

Joyce put a variant formulation in the enthusiastic but naive young voice of Stephen Dedalus:

> Welcome, O life! I go to encounter for the millionth time the reality of experience and to forge in the smithy of my soul the uncreated conscience of my race. [*Portrait*]

Joyce, as ever, was conscious of the ironies on the word 'forge'. Yeats was perhaps unconscious of the limitations of his use of the term 'fellow workers', to mean only those who worked in theatre or literature.

It is worth pursuing, very briefly, the contrast and comparison with the slum-dwelling Joyce, a 'fellow worker' remote from the imagined and real privileges of Coole Park.

The affirmation of everyone's potential equality had found a new mode of expression in that characteristic genre of the epoch of radical egalitarianism: the autobiography, a term from the decade of the French Revolution. Henceforth, it can seem, everybody has at least one book to write, the book of their own life, a portrait of the author as young. But another logic then emerges. Once that book is written, it too becomes simply another ordinary publication. To produce the truly special book, in this post-Romantic logic, is to produce the radically new, the summation and transcendence of all that precedes, from Homer to Meredith, from Sophocles to Ibsen. But, even then, logic demands another step: the cosmic text, the summation of everything, the book in which Here Comes Everybody, in which not even one's own language retains its special character but all languages are equal and language itself is made anew. Yeats' *A Vision*, too, has a certain affinity with this trajectory.

As I have argued elsewhere, Joyce's work seems to me caught in this logic, from the moment that he presented his own starting point in *Dubliners*. It can seem a radically individualist stance and creed: a relation between the equal but single individual and the cosmos itself, without mediation of nation or class; a curiously abstract soul under socialism. But, as Joyce's *Ulysses* insists, the normal logic of life is not individual but social, a matter of love and marriage in one of its many forms, and though Joyce and Nora refused the specific institutional form available in Catholic Ireland, *Ulysses* was to celebrate a married couple, ordinary in their everydayness — and as such it would be another contribution to changing a 'moral history' in which Parnell had been destroyed because of an everyday variation on marriage.

A year after Joyce's *Portrait* appeared, W. B. Yeats was also finally married, but not to his long-intended Maud Gonne. In what must have seemed an extraordinary example of moral luck, his marriage promptly provided him with his own cosmic work, and not through the dedicated obsessional labours of Joyce's *Wake*. Georgie Hyde-Lees' automatic writing seemed, to Yeats, to have brought what the whole world was awaiting: a new perspective upon the whole of history, an ultimate Vision. On the final page or so of *A Portrait,* in his diary entry for April 6th, Stephen acknowledges that other presence:

> Michael Robartes remembers forgotten beauty and, when his arms wrap her round, he presses in his arms the loveliness which has long faded from the world. Not this. Not at all. I desire to press in my arms the loveliness which has not yet come into the world.

In 1921 Yeats published a new volume of poems, entitled *Michael Robartes and the Dancer*, which was to revolve around both marriage, the choice and chance of love, and history, the choice and chance of politics, but also the cosmic and epochal. And the volume finally included the poem of that now extra-ordinary day, 'Easter 1916'. But if part of what is involved in our assessing Yeats' claims for himself, and with it the applicability of notions of moral luck, it is important to recognise how extra-ordinary those claims were. What was at stake was not simply the survival of a house or the emergence of a nation but a cosmic message for mankind.

choice and chance

Michael Robartes and the Dancer takes its title from the opening poem, a dialogue, which begins:

> He: Opinion is not worth a rush;
> In this altar-piece the knight,
> Who grips his long spear so to push
> That dragon through the fading light,
> Loved the lady; and it's plain
> The half-dead dragon was her thought,
> That every morning rose again
> And dug its claws and shrieked and fought.
> Could the impossible come to pass
> She would have time to turn her eyes,
> Her lover thought, upon the glass
> And on the instant would grow wise.

A female voice speaks next, but in what tone do we hear or perform it? What is her attitude? And then what is his?

She: You mean they argued.
He: Put it so;
But bear in mind your lover's wage
Is what your looking glass can show,
And that he will turn green with rage
At all that is not pictured there.
She: May I not put myself to college?

One might ask: who's winning? The initial response is the crucial one. After all his voluble interpretation of the painting, she responds, interrupts perhaps, with a mildly sarcastic put-down. She has to translate into simple intelligibility what he has so laboriously been saying. Her tone sets the tone of the battle between Michael Robartes and the Dancer, echoing the battle between the knight and the dragon; but the interpretation he offers is that the lady is outside the battle, *hors de combat.* The knight fights the dragon and the dragon is her thought, but she herself is relegated to the sidelines. His job is to suppress her thought. So she presumably does not reply to him as simply a thoughtful prompter: 'Oh, you mean they argued, that's what you've been saying.' The edge of saracasm is surely there in the voice required. He is then back on the defensive, though he tries to ride over her again. The crucial thing for women, he asserts, is how they look. And again the tone of her response is surely sarcastic. The poem and the volume, is now under way. But why begin the volume with this exchange?

We have just opened a book, and on the first page of that book we are told not only that 'Opinion is not worth a rush' but that:

. . what mere book can grant a knowledge
With an impassioned gravity
Appropriate to that beating breast,
That vigorous thigh, that dreaming eye?

And the book, it is clear, gives us only words, words on a page, which are several times removed, it seems, from any direct impassioned breast: a written version of a speech offering an interpretation of a painting of a story in which a knight fights a dragon, itself only an allegory —according to the offered interpretation. But then we find, towards the end of the poem:

> He: I have principles to prove me right.
> It follows from this Latin text
> That blest souls are not composite..

How can a Latin text, or even a poetic text, prove anything, if the poem has just dismissed knowledge from books? And what does 'Blest souls are not composite' even mean?

We might take it that 'blest souls' are not made up of separate elements, and women have the option, or at least the possibility, of living in blessed-ness if they will banish every thought, for what destroys un-compositeness is thinking, unless that thinking is itself somehow comprised within the very physical lineaments which constitute their beauty and their lover's desire. No wonder 'They say such different things at school'.

But this poem is itself composed of elements: we are given a dialogue, a composite, a poem in two voices, two parts, he and she, pro and anti, an argument and a riposte. Can we perform or think the poem in such a way that it is non-composite: not even a thought separable from the poem, but the whole poem as that thought? Can we read the poem itself without reducing it to allegory? Can the poem create the impassioned gravity that the poem itself demands as the condition for blessedness? Can the reader, in the effort of full response, somehow bring together Michael Robartes—words, intellect, books, the wise man, the old magician, the chauvinist—and the dancer, the girl, the young and beautiful, the flesh, those lineaments in the looking glass? If not, perhaps the world starts to fall apart, the centre cannot hold: you can either think or you can enjoy life, you can either be beautiful or you can be wise, you can either ride to harriers or you can take part in politics, you can perfect the life or the work—but you can never bring it all together. That is what is being introduced as the problematic for the whole of the volume, into which 'Easter 1916' is inserted.

The next poem, 'Solomon and the Witch', includes another dialogue of man and woman, though it also includes another, unattributed voice:

> And thus declared that Arab lady:
> 'Last night, where under the wild moon
> On grassy mattress I had laid me,
> Within my arms great Solomon,
> I suddenly cried out in a strange tongue
> Not his, not mine. '
> Who understood
> Whatever has been said, sighed, sung, etc.

We are plunged into the middle of a story, and into the middle of a problem. Solomon, famous for solving problems and for interpreting tongues, offers an explanation of Sheba's mysterious cry:

> A cockerel
> Crew from a blossoming apple bough
> Three hundred years before the Fall,
> And never crew again till now,
> And would not now but that he thought,
> Chance being at one with Choice at last,
> All that the brigand apple brought
> And this foul world were dead at last.
> He that crowed out eternity
> Thought to have crowed it in again . .

The cock thinks that what began the world has almost repeated itself, a conjunction of choice and chance. But why should that either begin or end the world? Choice is the option of doing one thing rather than another, while Chance is a matter of this happening rather than that. Can those two descriptions ever fully coincide without one account ceasing to apply? Is that what we used to call 'fate' —and do I perhaps choose my fate? Most people in this culture will get married to someone. Will whom you marry be a matter of chance, or a matter of choice?

If the world was so structured that our choices were always matched by our chances, our personal preferences always met by our opportunities, what kind of a world would that be? And yet what kind of a world is it, now, if it not so structured? If history is always what has finally happened, if the equation always balances to give the actual and only the actual as its result, then everything is predetermined and time is a kind of illusion. Eternity is only a realm of apparent possibilities where things may seem able to change but cannot really: they are simply and inescapably there, all the time. Yet we construct space and time by our seeking, hunting, travelling, moving—and we do so in the hope that what we find will match our expectations, preferences, and desires. If the world were so structured, after all, that there was no fissure between choice and chance, if they really were 'one at last', that would mean the end of expectation, hope, anticipation, even desire itself; it would indeed be the end of the world, as we know it.

The cock crows prematurely, in the poem. But why is it that even in this exceptional encounter of Solomon and Sheba —Sheba the most beautiful woman in legend and Solomon the wisest man—there still isn't a coincidence of choice and chance? If the conjunction were ever to occur, it would surely be here. Yet the normal conditions of love seem inescapable:

> Maybe the bride-bed brings despair
> For each an imagined image brings
> And finds a real image there;
> Yet the world ends when these two things,
> Though several, are a single light,
> When oil and wick are burned in one..

Again, a matter of trying to achieve uncomposite-ness, the urge for fusing apparent dichotomies into one-ness, a two into a one. But unsuccessfully:

> Maybe an image is too strong
> Or maybe is not strong enough.

Sheba's response is the emphatic urge to 'try again", and the pun is almost outrageous: they will attempt a second coming . . But notions of 'again' and 'second' are, after all, only possible in time. While they remain possible, 'the world stays", in time.

The issues of choice and chance remain. The next poem picks up 'image' in the title: 'An Image from a Past Life', and now it is, almost explicitly, Yeats and his wife, not Solomon and Sheba, who are the subject of the problem: choice or chance? But look first at the poem which comes immediately between 'An Image' and 'Easter 1916'. Why did Yeats put a poem dated 'November 1919' immediately before a poem entitled 'Easter 1916'? Is it simply a deliberate putting into dis-array any chronological notions of history? Or does this placing help us make sense of all three poems? 'Under Saturn' is again addressed to his wife and seems at first concerned only with another 'past image":

> Do not because this day I have grown saturnine
> Imagine that lost love, inseparable from my thought
> Because I have no other youth, can make me pine:
> For how should I forget that wisdom that you brought,
> The comfort that you made? . . .

This is a reminder, at one level, that history is always lived, remorselessly: being in history is a matter of having had this youth, and only this youth, including its actual choices and chances. The consolatory lines that follow seems at first merely a kind of tender self-excuse. But then what of these quite extraordinarily charged lines:

You heard that labouring man who had served my people
He said
Upon the open road, near to the Sligo quay —
No, no, not said, but cried it out—'You have come again,
And after twenty years it was time to come. '

The lines are given their electric charge partly by the same device that is used in 'Easter 1916': the repeated 'No, no, not . . but . .' ('No, no, not night but death"). The effect here is that we as readers almost have to 'cry out' the last part of the line: 'You have come again!' We cannot read this line except as a cry. And it's bound to echo the one cry the cock has already given, and Sheba's sudden cry in a language she couldn't understand. The overtones seem absolutely deliberate: the labouring man isn't merely welcoming Yeats back to Sligo. The echoes are apocalyptic: it was, after all, the Christ who was to 'come again".

This is immediately followed by the opening lines of 'Easter 1916":

I have met them at close of day
Coming with vivid faces...

Another coming? A false apocalypse?

And after we have read 'Easter 1916', in the exact organisation of this whole volume, we meet that quite explicit title: 'The Second Coming':

Turning and turning in the widening gyre
The falcon cannot hear the falconer;
Things fall apart; the centre cannot hold . .

Surely some revelation is at hand;
Surely the Second Coming is at hand.
The Second Coming! . .

Then notice the quite extraordinary juxtaposition at the end of 'Second Coming':

For now I know that twenty centuries of stony sleep
Were vexed to nightmare by a rocking cradle,
And what rough beast, its hour come round at last,
Slouches towards Bethlehem to be born?

Within the volume this is immediately followed by:

A Prayer for my Daughter

Once more the storm is howling, and half hid
Under this cradle-hood and coverlid
My child sleeps on . .

A terrible beauty is born, indeed! The associations between this newly born daughter, the birth of a new era, the second coming, the conjunction of choice and chance, seem inescapable: they are either incredibly unconscious or unbelievably deliberate. We remember that other question from 'Under Saturn':

For how should I forget the wisdom that you brought . . ?

For what else had happened to Yeats in this curious historical moment, of his marriage and the birth of his daughter? The ''wisdom' that had been brought into the marriage had been that extraordinary stream of automatic writing which was to be the basis of *A Vision.* Yeats first announced the event to Lady Gregory in a letter of October 29th 1917:

> There has been something very like a miraculous intervention. Two days ago I was in great gloom (of which I hope, and believe, George knew nothing). I was saying to myself 'I have betrayed three people'; then I thought 'I have lived all through this before.' Then George spoke of the sensation of having lived through something before (she knew nothing of my thought). Then she said she felt that something was to be written through her. She got a piece of paper, and talking to me all the while so that her

> thoughts would not affect what she wrote, she wrote these words . . .

Yeats gave a more public account in *A Vision* itself:

> On the afternoon of October 24th, 1917, four days after my marriage, my wife surprised me by attempting automatic writing. What came in disjointed sentences, in almost illegible writing, was so exciting, sometimes so profound, that I persuaded her to give an hour or so day after day to the unknown writer, and after some half dozen such hours offered to spend what remained of life explaining and piecing together those scattered sentences. 'No' was the answer, "we have come to give you metaphors for poetry. '

Remember the context of that marriage. For twenty years or more, Yeats had pursued Maud Gonne, and had been refused, again and again. Then he had pursued Iseult Gonne, and again been refused. Finally, in what must have seemed from the outside very much like a third or fourth choice, hardly even a choice, more a sort of acquiescence in chance, he had married Georgina Hyde-Lees. And—quite unexpectedly—this matching of Yeats and Georgina had, it seemed, produced a vision, a revelation, the truth, perhaps the second coming, a wisdom to rival Solomon's. By then, Yeats was, or could see himself as, the senior surviving Master of the Order of the Golden Dawn. All his early mages, his occult teachers, his wisdom masters, had been exposed as frauds, or fallen away or died—leaving William Butler Yeats as not only the great poet, the craftsman with words, but also as the sole special recipient of the hidden knowledge, the revelation so long awaited, and so long promised within the occult societies to which he had remained attached and faithful. Finally, he was, after all, to be the medium through which Truth was to enter the world.

The nearly explicit megalomania is staggering. But if it were to be regarded as true, both the events and *a fortiori* the poem of 'Easter 1916' would be placed within a much wider perspective, as an occasion of relatively minor importance. Easter 1916 itself would be only one of a number of events, signs and signals of an utter transformation: everything changed, changed utterly.

It's hard to comprehend, let alone endorse, such a perspective. Yet it's worth remembering that from a quite other perspective, at precisely that same historical moment, it could indeed be claimed that the whole of human history had taken a decisive turn, that it had been transformed, or was at least in the initial stages of an utter transformation — at this determinate historical moment in October-November 1917. The revelations started to happen to Yeats on October 24th 1917. The crucial turning point of the Russian Soviet Revolution was the meeting of the second All-Russian Congress of Soviets on the evening of October 25th 1917. The decisive take-over of power by the Bolsheviks occurred over the next few days. Some would still hold to the perspective opened up by that decisive event, even if few of us can even make sense of Yeats's similarly decisive claim to a new epochal beginning. We are perhaps more inclined to extend Yeats's own hypothesis, in the letter to Lady Gregory:

> I had begun to believe just before my marriage that I had acted . . because my mind was unhinged by strain.

A whole generation had, however, adopted a similar perspective upon the new century. In Nietzsche, there had been the glimpse of a trans-valuation of all values. The thought had perhaps helped to drive him mad: the notion that all the values by which the civilisation of which they were part claimed to be governed—truth, mercy, charity, forgiveness—were clearly bankrupt and that what was to replace them was to be brutality, force, violence, the will to power, sheer struggle for mastery, an epoch of harshness and cruelty and violence, a naked struggle for supremacy.

In that context, how was one to respond, how was one to understand the shape of that moment?

In some respects, the best poem for grasping the structure of the world-view made explicit in *A Vision* is 'Demon and Beast', placed immediately before 'The Second Coming':

For certain minutes at the least
That crafty demon and that loud beast
That plague me day and night
Ran out of my sight;
Though I had long perned in the gyre,
Between my hatred and desire,
I saw my freedom won
And all laugh in the sun.

Clearly, another dragon, though no longer simply a painted one. A clear parallel is set up between demon and beast and hatred and desire. One could paraphrase the sense: that having been shuttled back and forth between hatred and desire, those object-related emotions and intensities for power, suddenly the freedom, the liberation, comes accidentally, arbitrarily, by chance, and very temporarily, for certain minutes (but minute by minute we change).

The second stanza takes us into the context of the art gallery ('To a wealthy man. .'), including those historical figures now embalmed into art.

Now that the loud beast ran
There was no portrait in the Gallery
But beckoned to sweet company,
For all men's thoughts grew clear
Being dear as mine are dear

But then the movement of the poem begins to turn against itself, to spiral in a different direction, to change:

But soon a teardrop started up
For aimless joy had made me stop
Beside the little lake
To watch a white gull take
A bit of bread thrown up into the air;
Now gyring down and perning there

He splashed where an absurd
Portly green-pated bird
Shook off the water from his back;
Being no more demoniac
A stupid happy creature
Could rouse my whole nature.

This absence of hatred and of desire, the absence of objects of passion, leaves one with an object-less aim-lessness: a matter of drifting chance. We are back in that world of a horse plashing on the brim, of everything that changes minute by minute. Here, for a few minutes, aimless joy and a bird gyring down, that echo of the earlier 'I had long perned in the gyre." It is the bird now that is caught in the spiralling movement, circling down to catch the passing object of its desire, the casual, trivial bread.

Being no more demoniac
A stupid happy creature
Could rouse my whole nature.

Yes—and no. The creature's happiness seems related to its stupidity, its mere animality. Therefore, the notion that it could arouse the whole nature of the speaker in the poem strains our credulity. And indeed the poem disconfirms it, as another counter-movement of the poem round its own psychological and emotional spiral now begins.

Yet I am certain as can be
That every natural victory
Belongs to beast or demon . .

Mastery comes from hatred or desire, from the beast or demon. Notice, though, that this certainty perhaps echoes another and dubious certainty, from 'Easter 1916' ("being certain that they and I but lived where motley is worn'). The certainty here continues, into:

. . That mere growing old, that brings
Chilled blood, this sweetness brought.

Yet have no dearer thought
Than that I may find out a way
To make it linger half a day.

Again, 'Yet' signals the beginning of a counter-movement. The words 'sweet' and '"dear' are taking on several different connotations and resonances within the poem and the volume ('how daring and sweet', '"what voice more sweet", 'for all men's thoughts grew dear'). The desire that now comes into operation is the desire for remaining in that state of aimlessness, even though the momentary certainties have produced a two-fold disconfirmation of that desire: such aimlessness is not mastery but mere ageing, not a recipe for achievement but merely a kind of emptiness.

The poem has thereby enacted a kind of spiralling or gyring movement, as it shifts from moment to moment, each change the consequence but also the cancelling of the previous position. The poem constructs the gyring and perning movement which, at the psychological level, Yeats saw as the inescapable pattern of a life, and which on a broader scale he also saw as giving shape to the fundamental transformations, the epochal changes, of history. Which the poem finally arrives at:

Oh what a sweetness strayed
Through barren Thebaid,
Or by the Mareotic sea
When that exultant Anthony
And twice a thousand more
Starved upon the shore
And withered to a bag of bones!
What had the Ceasars but their thrones?

That conjunction of Caesar and Anthony makes us, unavoidably, by an anticipated confusion, think of Antony and Cleopatra, that meeting of desires, and of choice and chance, but also of war: the working through of a conflict of hatreds, of opposition, of struggle for mastery.

Those characters and events are still resonances and points of referemce, terms of intelligibility, as we think through the epoch that is ending. Yet what the stanza actually refers to is a quite different domain, a different cultural framework. The Anthony is Saint Anthony, the first hermit, who went out into the desert to fast, to starve, and to pray. We are no longer able easily or fully to make sense of the actions of those first hermits. We think of them as seeking spiritual solace, or peace and quiet, the conditions for personal sancitity. We forget, or fail to grasp, and cannot fully imagine, that in their own eyes they went out into the desert to combat the demon, to occupy the terrain given over to the devil, to struggle not only against the wild beasts but also against the beast within and those who were masters of the wild beasts and the wild spaces, the demons.

In *Macbeth* or in *Lear*, on the heath, in the waste-land, we can still catch some echoes of that earlier belief-system. Witches, evil, madness, that which lies beyond rationality and beyond morality, occupies the barren Thebaid, the Mareotic sea. Through the action of this movement of the spirit, this conquest of the desert, civilisation advanced beyond the tiny glimmerings of light in the grim dark which we call cities and began to inhabit, make habitable and human, those far spaces. That was a different kind of battle from Caesar's, fuelled by a different kind of desire from Antony's, and yielding a quite different kind of sweetness, almost unimaginable today.

But it's the consequences of that movement into the desert which arguably gave a shape to an whole epoch. Christian civilisation rested upon the maintenance, against the power of the darkness and the devil, of the light of the world. But the poem has ended upon this moment partly because if we are to enter upon a new stage, not only at the level of the individual psyche but in the historical epoch itself, it may be that we will enter a world where the old values—the present ones—will themselves become unimaginable and inconceivable, not so much forgotten as incomprehensible:

Turning and turning in the widening gyre
The falcon cannot hear the falconer;
Things fall apart, the centre cannot hold;
Mere anarchy is loosed upon the world,
The blood-dimmed tide is loosed, and everywhere
The ceremony of innocence is drowned;
The best lack all conviction, while the worst
Are full of passionate intensity.

If that is to be the case, or is already the case, it is important that this marriage of Yeats and Georgina which has already produced the revelation, the insight into those conditions, has also resulted in a different kind of birth, a fusion of two into one, a new composite, possibly a truly blest soul: a baby daughter lies sleeping, but amid a demonic howl.

And for an hour I have walked and prayed
Because of the great gloom that is in my mind.

But what kind of prayer does one pray as the Christian epoch ends?

I have walked and prayed for this young child an hour
And heard the sea-wind scream upon the tower,
And under the arches of the bridge, and scream
In the elms above the flooded stream;

Again those screams, now not only from Juno's peacock, or from Sheba in her mysterious cry, or the crow of the cock, or the crying out of the labouring man. But now a harsher, edgier scream, the scream of sufferings to come:

Imagining in excited reverie
That the future years had come,
Dancing to a frienzied drum,
Out of the murderous innocence of the sea.

In this new world, far from brave:

May she be granted beauty and yet not
Beauty to make a stranger's eye distraught,
Or hers before a looking-glass . . .

We are taken back to that first exchange in the volume, between Michael Robartes and the dancer. The notion there, of a beautiful woman gazing into a looking-glass and confirming in it the possibility of a kind of thought, of passionate intensity, is here denied. Equally, let the daughter beware now even of the attractions of choice:

Helen being chosen found life flat and dull
And later had much trouble from a fool,
While that great Queen, that rose out of the spray,
Being fatherless could have her way
Yet chose a bandy-legged smith for man.

The volume returns to the refusal of certain kinds of value, of intellect, even of beauty itself. The poem ends with an old affirmation:

. . . may her bridegroom bring her to a house
Where all's accustomed, ceremonious . . .

Is that groom to be a matter of choice or of chance, and is this house perhaps already shaken by new agitations? And whence can come this accustomed ceremoniousness if even the ceremony of innocence is drowned?

For arrogance and hatred are the wares
Peddled in the thoroughfares.
How but in custom and in ceremony
Are innocence and beauty born?

Again a birth, but not a rough beast, nor even a terrible beauty. Innocence and beauty. How but in ceremony? The poem as a whole has no answer to that quasi-rhetorical query. But if the world is to change, to change utterly, it cannot be a merely rhetorical question: the new conditions for its answer are unthinkable within the categories of the old epoch. There is a kind of reversion here to the world of Coole Park, but now placed within a fragile, temporary, threatened environment:

> There is no obstacle
> But Gregory's wood and one bare hill
> Whereby the haystack- and roof-levelling wind,
> Bred on the Atlantic can be stayed . . .

In the great gloom that is in his mind, all thought of the future, even of his daughter's future, can become only a kind of entrenched defence.

The final poem of the volume seeks refuge and a form of permanence, a defence against more than the wind:

> To Be Carved on a Stone at Thoor Ballylee
>
> I, the poet William Yeats,
> With old mill boards and sea-green slates,
> And smithy work from the Gort forge,
> Restored this tower for my wife George;
> And may these characters remain
> When all is ruin once again.

No longer an eighteenth century country house, a shooting lodge, or a cultural oasis, but a fortified Norman Tower, itself a kind of survivor from a previous change and transformation. One may not get knowledge or wisdom from a book; the books themselves, as fragile printed objects, may not even survive: we can turn to the tower, to the ruin, to those incised characters upon the stone, like ancient runes. One day, they will be ancient runes. Minute by minute, things change. But this stone, when all is ruin once again, and again, and again, will perhaps remain. The stone is still in the midst of all.

And when, and if, that stone itself is destroyed, cracked, grown over, illegible, these 'characters' may yet remain, detached from context, released from history, escaping the equation of the actual. To be read now, here, not in their time and place but in mine, and yours. Phrases remembered. What we call literature.

But where does 'literature' come from?

Let us return to our poem.

reading a poem II

> It is a known fact that a commentary is something different from a carefully weighed appreciation apportioning light and shade. The commentary proceeds from the classic nature of its text and hence, as it were, from a prejudgement. (Walter Benjamin)

> *Qua* work of art, the work of art cannot be interpreted; there is nothing to interpret . . for 'interpretation' the chief task is the presentation of relevant historical facts which the reader is not assumed to know. (T. S. Eliot)

My extended 'commentary' upon this single 'minor' poem by Yeats has not been an 'interpretation' of that poem, in the sense of elucidating what its words mean, or even, in any important sense, what Yeats might have meant by the poem. I do not believe the poem is likely to require any such 'interpretation' for my readers. Nor have I simply tried to offer historical 'facts' which would be 'relevant' to interpreting what the words, or Yeats, meant. And the 'historical facts' I have deployed have not primarily been chosen as ones that I assumed you, as reader, would not know.

I have nevertheless operated from a pre-judgement, indeed from the assumption of a pre-judgement on your own part also. But not a prejudgement about the aesthetic or literary merit of this poem. What my commentary has aimed to do is simply to provoke, stimulate, or make apparent, a fuller awareness of what is involved in the response to the poem which I have prejudged you as having already made. In that sense I have taken a gamble, a not uncommon one for a critic. And by trying to make explicit what I believe is already involved in the responses which I assume, I have been in danger of simply burying the poem under the weight, and extent, of the commentary.

That last danger, however, also indicates what seems to me an important feature of reading that is often forgotten, or found no place for, in literary criticism.

Our actual responses to a poem are considerably more complex and multi-layered than the terms 'interpretation' or 'evaluation' allow. As we read, we bring into play several interacting layers of response, some fully conscious but others barely glimpsed at the margins of our minds and memory, some recognised as immediately and directly 'relevant', others hardly acknowledged before being quickly dismissed, yet naggingly felt to connect, somehow. The sheer speed with which we move through these operations of response, recall, and reference, is very difficult to reproduce in any critical 'analysis'. Our reading, as it actually happens, can involve registers of emotional reaction we almost instantly repress, or perhaps 'purely personal' resonances we both repudiate as 'irrelevant' yet also insist upon retaining, obscurely aware that what they offer is cognate—though we can't quite say how or why—with what the poem includes and invites. I have therefore tried, in the commentary, to admit and make explicit some of these half-caught layers of response.

In particular, my commentary has relied upon one fleeting and perhaps repressed response which I am assuming that you as reader will also have made in reading the poem: a half recognition that the reader too is implicated in the question of the poem. More specifically, I have assumed that this response will have been present in your reaction to the information about Sir William Gregory and the Gregory Clause, in relation to the phrase 'gifts that govern men'. If you admitted—at however latent or implicit a level—that a judgement upon Sir William Gregory was indeed part of, or had now become part of, your actual response to the poem, then the 'logic' of my commentary could get under way.

In one sense, the specific 'facts' I offered about the Gregory Clause are not essential to my point; those facts could have been more or less different, or other facts could have served just as well. It might have been the case, for example, that it was Sir William's father who was responsible for the Gregory Clause, while Sir William himself had died while ministering to the victims of famine fever (which is how his father, on one account, did actually die). My information on Ceylon may have been unreliable. Lady Gregory's income might have been, in today's terms, £10,000 or £500,000. The precise and limited point I am making here is that my commentary assumes only a recognition of the relevance not only of such facts but also of one's own moral response to them in responding to the poem.

I can now draw out some general implications from the overall commentary. In quoting Bakhtin's remark that 'In no instance is the extraverbal situation only an external cause of the utterance' I commented:

> The extraverbal situation of my citing this poem is, among other things, this writing and your reading. How can that be involved in the very 'understanding' of Yeats's text? What question, and what embryo of an answer, is thereby involved, for us both?

Let me now suggest at least the embryo of an answer.

Two factors seem to be involved in the extra-verbal situation of this commentary. To spend time trying to disentangle the various layers of response involved in reading this poem, to pursue allegedly relevant historical facts through long, sometimes unappealing, passages from a variety of possibly unfamiliar kinds of source, to try to follow quite complex arguments in economic theory or moral philosophy, to dwell upon and attempt to associate such divers matters as an art gallery in Cambridge and Tamil tea-workers in Sri Lanka, a lunch in Venice and the rise of US capitalism, Gauguin's exile and the 1916 Easter Rising

—to spend time on all this—indicates two things: that you, as reader, are sufficiently engaged by or involved in the problem of this way of trying to 'understand' the poem (rather than, say, wanting simply a literary appreciation of it) to have continued thus far; and, secondly and crucially, that in order to be able to do so, you are almost certainly in a situation of considerable comparative privilege.

Neither of these points will need much spelling out for you —but I am trying to make implications as explicit as possible. The points I have made also apply, even more, to myself as writer of what you have been reading. The second point is easier to specify. Anyone who has the time, facilities and education to write or read this text enjoys conditions of existence that are enormously privileged, probably in terms of most local comparisons, and certainly in terms of any global frame of reference. To be able to find the time, space, and relative peace and quiet, necessary for writing or reading this exercise, and to be able to concentrate one's energies and attention for a few hours upon a single minor poem of Yeats is to be in a very small minority indeed. However, to use that time and that privilege to try to recognise how that poem is itself related to a certain global history and global distribution of privilege, is at least to acknowledge a question about one's own relative privilege, a question which other modes of analysing, evaluating or commenting upon the poem would not necessarily raise.

Combining these two factors, one can clearly see — and this is the fundamental response I have pre-judged and expanded upon — elements of a shared situation with the Yeats of the poem itself. What enables this kind of 'understanding' (which takes the form of an embryonic answer to a question, a reply to, rather than an interpretation of, the poem) is not some shared knowledge of Sligo topography but more like a recognition of being oneself in a situation which has a structural similarity to that which the poem deals with—as Peter Ure might have recognised a relation between his situation in Greece and some of the issues raised by Yeats' work.

Any reader of this poem thereby confronts, one can suggest, a 'moral luck' decision, of considerable complexity. It would be too simple to invoke notions of 'guilt' at this point, to say that what is principally involved in my account of this poem is a feeling of guilt about my own privileged position. That is certainly worth saying, or admitting, but it does not take us very far. Part of the point of trying to un-pack the full dimensions of my (and your?) response is to indicate just how inadequate a simple recourse to the vocabulary of guilt is, and how incomplete it is as an answer or reply, even in the familiar form of self-accusation.

Why 'guilt' is too simple, and use-less, a term is partly indicated by the fact that I would most certainly defend the conditions of relative privilege which I enjoy (even if I did not enjoy them), as a university teacher, against the present government policy of reducing expenditure on universities and whittling away the legal securities university teachers have traditionally had.

The form of the defence would not, only, be Yeats's response to those who refused to spend Dublin Corporation money on an art gallery: that he respected the argument that the money might be otherwise better spent on slum clearance, but despised those who deployed that argument in the knowledge that it would not be so spent. Nor would my defence involve claiming that each and every item of university expenditure, or every form of university privilege, was justified: it would certainly involve an argument about the level of financial reduction that would render a university 'too ruinous' to perform its task.

But the essential defence would have itself to take the form of a moral luck argument, akin to that at the basis of Yeats's poem on the art gallery: that the justification for maintaining the relative privileges, the very conditions of existence, of a university rests upon the future which that university will, retrospectively, be judged to have enabled. By its very nature, that argument is a slippery one, yet it has to be the essential argument deployed from any position which acknowledges that a moral cost is indeed involved in any privilege, even one mediated by and only effectively located in an institution.

I recognise, therefore, that many —though not all—of the issues raised around Coole Park earlier also apply to the university in which I work and without which I would not have the conditions of privilege which enable that work. Most of my readers are likely to have, or to have had, some such privilege.

There are, of course, differences between Coole Park and a university: my university is not a privately-owned home, but a publicly funded institution (so far), yet as an important employer of local non-academic labour, as an investor, as a recipient of—in one sense—'unearned income', through the tax system and central government funding, that university is in a relation of financial power to many of the people who work for it and of financial indebtedness to many who, it can seem, derive no benefit themselves from it.

Though a university may seem to be far more 'pure' or one-dimensionally functional, by comparison with the multiple facets of a Coole Park, by the very fact of its being a material institution—a set of buildings requiring maintenance, people requiring 'catering', accommodation, cleaning services, etc.—a university cannot be regarded only in terms of an analysis of its apparently dominant functions. The University of Liverpool, I am told, is now the largest single employer within the inner boundaries of that once prosperous city. The city's motto, incidentally, is '*Deus haec nobis otia fecit*'—'God has given us this leisure, these benefits' —a divine gift, then, rather than, say, the slave trade which underpinned the city's wealth

Nor can the contribution of Coole Park to the 'governing' of other people, and peoples, be used to differentiate Coole neatly from, say, the University of Kent, where I work. Universities are clearly designed, in part, to facilitate the 'gifts that govern' others, and have historically had that role. Just as with Coole Park, therefore, the task of 'justifying' a university rests upon a complex interplay of judgements about its past, its specific characteristics, its probable future and those of its students—but involved in all such judgements are not only explicit and arguable criteria (whether, for example, the place does or does not combine 'passion and precision', 'high laughter' with 'loveliness' — though it would be rather pleasant if some did), but also quite definite 'political' choices, about who benefits, and who governs. The class composition of the student intake in British universities is a sharp reminder of the continuing politics of these choices.

It is not, therefore, a merely idiosyncratic response that allows a shift, a certain slide, in my own reading of 'Upon a House', from 'this house' as referring to Coole Park to 'this house' as referring, in a shadowing way, to 'this' or any other university. If I am unable to justify the hypothetical protection of Coole Park from the land agitation, I may also be unable, in quite practical terms, to justify my own conditions of work. Conversely, if I contemplate the preservation of Coole, I may have to come to terms with what such preservation really involves in the case of my own institution. The 'shifter' effect of such demonstratives as 'this' and 'that' in Yeats's poetry can operate with considerable effect:

> How can I, that girl standing there . .
>
> ('Politics')

> That is no country for old men . .
>
> ('Sailing to Byzantium')

In the case of 'Upon a House' the shift of implicit reference which I acknowledge in my own reading of the poem is built upon a structural similarity of situation, rather than upon any simple ambiguity of reference. And underlying this linguistic reflexivity is perhaps an endorsement of Yeats's remark that 'out of the quarrel with ourselves we make poetry', and a perception of that 'quarrel' not merely in emotional or passional terms, but as generated by a structural contradiction, a social impasse.

marginal intellectuals

Yet it may well be asked why a mapping of my own position onto that underlying Yeats's poem should be of any interest, or relevance, to other readers. I have already suggested that most readers of this book will, in two crucial respects, share that over-mapping, that their—your, or our—own situation will be, to some extent, analysable along the same lines. The point could be put in a familiar rhetoric: that, of course, this poem appeals in a masochistic way to 'marginalised intellectuals', 'marginalised' by their incapacity to make any substantial contribution to the 'real' problems of economic development, and 'intellectuals' because they retain a privileged commitment to such pursuits as writing and reading books on Yeats, who was also (so the circle closes) himself a marginalised intellectual in the Ireland of the 1910s, unable to contribute any solution to the problems of landownership or of agricultural reform, political agitation or armed insurrection, which were required by the historical situation. The model we should therefore adopt for ourselves is not Yeats but those other poets, academics and literary critics, Patrick Pearse and Thomas MacDonagh, who abandoned their careers as schoolmasters, or minor literary figures and university lecturers to take part in the Easter rising.

Yet before moving quite so quickly to that rhetoric, or to that further quarrel with others and with ourselves, it should be noted that the potential targets for that attack are now very numerous indeed. For the term 'marginalised intellectual' can now legitimately apply not just to university teachers of English, or to potential readers of this book, but also to a very large segment of the population of the developed countries.

Insofar as a characteristic and time-consuming activity of the people of Britain, America, Ireland, France, Germany, Japan, etc., is watching television (one requiring relative conditions of peace, quiet, leisure, affluence . .), that very activity also positions them (while pursuing it) very directly in a variant of the uncomfortable category of the 'marginalised intellectual'. For the central characteristic of television now is that it puts a whole globe, regularly, into our living rooms. We are spectators, potentially, of the entire world: we can, and do, sit and watch famine in sub-Sahara Africa, food mountains in EEC warehouses, airplane disasters in Japan, Mother Theresa in Calcutta, industrial pollution in Poland, dissidents in Beijing, hostages in Beirut (one bulletin's news items).

For the first time in human history, a quite large percentage of the human race can watch, even as they happen, events occurring across the whole globe, the entire planet. We can even see that whole globe itself spinning slowly in space. Since the Apollo 8 broadcast on Christmas Eve 1968 we have all had that image of the world as just another planet lurking in our memories. It is deeply characteristic of what that perspective implies that the famine in Ethiopia prompted, in 1985, a television 'event' watched by some 500 million people—and it is also symptomatic that the event was a concert of music, a 'cultural' event, an act of putative unification achieved by a contemporary version of 'writing it out in a verse'.

Yet the experience of watching the daily output of world news, and, most acutely, the experience of watching such events as Bob Geldof's *Live Aid* global juke-box, has been to drive home both the unavoidability of some 'moral' reaction to global events and a recognition of incapacity on the part of those watching to 'do' anything very substantial about those events. What television reinforces is a sense that most of us do not, most of the time, at all have the 'gifts' of 'governing' the events that we watch.

By its continual interviewing of 'professional' politicians and by its use of 'experts' (often drawn either from other branches of journalism or from academic institutions) for instant analysis and comment, but also, far more crucially, by its formal division—built into the current means and mode of transmission and reception—between those who might directly intervene and those who cannot, who can only sit and watch, or perhaps simply make a requested donation, a 'gift', television positions us all as marginalised; and yet, insofar as we watch, we see, we seek to understand, also as nascent 'intellectuals'.

And it is the very conditions of existence which enable us to watch in the first place that drive home to us the inescapability of a 'moral' response to our comparative privilege. It is the immediate juxtaposition of a starving child with, and visibly within, our own more or less affluent living room, also visible to us as we watch, that renders such devices as juxta-posing extracts about 1909 slums and journal entries about holiday lunches for royalty in Venice almost anachronistic. Today, the Venice luncheon party could actually be watching a starving child dying 'live' on their TV screens as they munched the cucumber sandwiches. Conversely, a child in a Palestinian refugee camp might be watching an Israeli State Banquet as it went hungry to bed.

The possibility of personally experiencing such sharp contrasts and juxtapositions has always been available to restricted categories of people, mainly to those who 'governed' and those who were professional 'intellectuals'. Until very recently, only a very small segment of the global population was able either to travel across the globe to see for themselves, or even, on any regular basis, to read reports of events in distant parts of the globe. Only a member of at least the Sir William Gregory stratum could winter in India, spend the spring in Spain, stop over in Egypt, could compare for themselves conditions in Calcutta and Killarney.

Every Empire, of course, has had its complement of administrators, civil servants, messengers, and military, who travelled between the metropolis and the outposts. Often the only form of foreign travel for working class individuals was as part of an invading or occupying power. But these remained a minority within the overall population. For the majority, of course, from the earliest days of news dissemination, from seamen's stories and pilgrims' tales, from travellers' reports to the electric telegraph, some opportunity to become aware of events far away has been available, but during almost exactly the period of Yeats's adult life a qualitative change occurred.

From, say, 1875 to 1939, we can date the emergence of a mass press, of film newsreels, the very beginnings of television, the extraordinary development of international communication by telephone and radio, the unprecedented acceleration and extension of regular travel by land, sea and air, but also perhaps the construction of a quite new conception of the notion of 'the world' itself.

Yeats, however, was not simply a passive observer of these global changes Precisely as an Irish writer he was in a position to register that qualitative change as directly affecting his own work, his own identity. It was not only that in his socially privileged contacts with the Gregorys or with British politicians and Prime Ministers, Yeats was aware of the extensive reach of those who 'governed' a quarter of the world, in a way not available to most of the population. Nor was it simply that as an Irish writer close to the movements for national independence, he was aware of the potentially global ramifications of that national self-assertion against a global Empire. Simply as a writer Yeats was confronted with one other global dimension: that the very language he chose to write in—against other possible and even pressing considerations—was now a world language.

Between 1860 and 1900 the British Empire had expanded territorially five-fold: by 1910, as the 1911 *Encyclopaedia Britannica* observed, that Empire covered a quarter of the world's land surface, 12 million square miles out of 52 million total. English was now an official language or a *lingua franca* (though the irony of that phrase should also register) for an extraordinary proportion of the world population, and unlike Chinese, or Spanish in Latin America, one that stretched into every imagined corner of the globe, from Canada to Ceylon, from Kenya to Kilkenny, from Capetown to Canberra, from Maine to Malaysia.

To have chosen *not* to write in English would have been to refuse the opportunity of writing for a literally world-wide audience. There were, of course, other quite decidedly practical reasons why, say, an Irish cottager from Connaught should have chosen English as the language of personal advance, especially those with an eye on emigration to America, and there were also serious counter-vailing arguments for a revival of Gaelic literature as a contribution to Irish national identity. That phrase in Yeats's poem, 'written speech' somewhat sidesteps the tangle of issues here.

But for Yeats—even apart from the fact that Gaelic would have been for him a 'second' language anyway—the considerations that led Douglas Hyde to write in Gaelic or even those that led Lady Gregory to 'translate' from Gaelic, were overwhelmed by the recognition that he, William Butler Yeats, was to aim for a status beyond that of a Hyde or a Gregory, a status precisely as a major poet, an international figure. And if part of the drive, or justification, impelling that ambition was a recognition that achieving that stature would be a contribution to Irish national identity—an awareness that the poetry of 'William Butler Yeats' would indeed serve to identify Ireland culturally for others and give her 'a place among the nations of the world'—then the very fact of writing in English offered him an avenue to that status and contribution that writing in no other language could have done.

Whatever the alleged merits or limits of English as a language for literature, whatever the ironic implications for Irish culture of writing in the language of the imperial power, English nevertheless had the unique advantage of being the world language. Whatever the other facets of the global history of British imperialism, that 'written speech' now spread throughout the world was indeed 'gradual Time's last gift'.

It was, therefore, in a significantly new and global frame of reference that Yeats's question could genuinely and not only rhetorically be asked:

How should the world be luckier . . . .

It is now a question that demands a reply every time we tune into a satellite transmission. The relation between the individual watcher and the whole globe is a peculiarly unmediated one—despite all the actual mediations built into the very media through which we encounter that globe. Arguably, if part of the task and project of Yeats was to become an 'Irish' poet, the task and project that now seems on the agenda for us all is to become post-national in our own identity, to become citizens of the world—a phrase another Irish English writer, Goldsmith, had once made his own.

But, of course, our relationship to the world at large necessarily begins from a specific location, a definite place, a home-town. And even if the airwaves are now saturated and the global images multiply, one question that still asks for an answer is the role of literature itself: what contribution can it now make to our common history? We can probe that question by looking back from a further perspective at what reading this poem might now mean for us, what questions it still invites us to answer, if only in embryo. Perhaps now on a larger scale?

interruptions

—Most of what you have been reading up to now was written in 1984-85. I drafted a conclusion at the time, but then put the book aside. Partly because —pursuing the logic of my own argument about the role of literature —I really did not think, by then, that working as a literary critic was as worthwhile or as useful as it had once seemed.

Accordingly, I more or less switched disciplines and concerns. For several years, I concentrated on the then rapidly developing field of multimedia computing. It is easy to forget, so swift have the changes been, that in the mid-1980s 'computers' were still largely main-frame monsters in air-conditioned special rooms, and the 'personal computer' was not only expensive but still largely limited to a machine which could only handle mathematical calculations, text-processing, and spreadsheets, and was programmed by writing line after line of intricate code. The emergence of the first Apple Macs, together with the arguably far more technically innovative and flexible Amiga and even Atari machines, enabled a relatively untrained user to learn, and perhaps write, programs which added image-processing, music composition and playback, sound recording and manipulation, and even—by the end of the decade—some basic digital video editing. It therefore seemed to me, in those years, that such developments offered enormous potential for change, social, cultural, and political, and even more so—as seemed just feasible in the '80s—when eventually combined with and integrated into the communications and media networks.

I therefore set up what I believe was the first UK Humanities-based university degree programme in these emerging areas, about which I have written elsewhere, and firmly put aside the academic teaching of 'literature'. However, in 1987, partly because I still had a somewhat unwelcome publishing commission to honour, but also as occasional relief from the intensive challenges of learning to master the constantly changing software and hardware in my new field, I tried to complete the Yeats piece, extending the original argument to take some account of what by then seemed to me important further aspects of the argument I had originally pursued.

What now follows in this book is, in part, the draft conclusion, written over a couple of weekends in late 1987. But at the end of the print-out from that date is a note to myself:

> 9th November 1987.
>
> I spent this past weekend trying to give some shape to this sprawling text, to reconcile and knit together the various layers of draft composition. Since I had the house to myself till Monday, I could concentrate entirely on the writing, so I avoided all distraction from television, radio, newspapers. In any case, I could guess at the likely content of the Sunday news—it was Remembrance Sunday—and it seemed somehow appropriate that I should spend that day trying to think through issues about how literature enables a curious kind of remembering, how it involves us in the complexities of past conflicts.

> —As usual, I wrote throughout the night on Sunday, and finally fell asleep feeling moderately pleased with the writing: the commentary sections are more or less completed, and the rest fairly fully drafted. Another full weekend and the piece might be finished.
> — I woke late this morning, Monday, and finally looked at the TV news. On Sunday the Remembrance Day gathering in Enniskillen, County Fermanagh, was devastated by a bomb. Eleven killed and sixty injured. Including a pregnant woman. The footage is horrifying.The bomb was apparently placed inside the town's Reading Rooms, a known vantage point for watching the parade.
> —It seems pointless and even heartless to continue with this excercise in mere literary criticism. If I thought that anything I could write would make some difference, I might complete it. But — Maybe some day.

There is a further printed note, stapled to a slightly longer second version of the print-out, which reads:

> August 1998
>
> It's now ten years since I put this in a drawer and decided to move out of 'literature' entirely. But with the Good Friday Agreement and the various ceasefires, it seemed that perhaps it was time to look again at what might be salvageable from this text. Just possibly, it might be useful to revive the attempt to link this peculiarly complex poem of August 1909 to the continuing issues I once tried to consider, not only those of Ireland but the global developments that were only sketched in what remains of the draft conclusion.
> —August 7th, the date of Yeats' orginal composition, seemed auspicious as a day on which to start again.
> —A week later, on August 15th, the Real IRA have exploded a bomb in Omagh. Twenty-nine people are dead. Whatever lingering optimism underpinned my exercise in trying to understand Yeats has dissolved again. Some other time. Perhaps.

It is now, as I write this, May 2015. The next 20 pages or so are what remains of that 1998 draft conclusion. It might take you twenty minutes to read them. There is then a final note at the end, to finish this still-unfinishable book, considering why I now publish it after all, and after all this time. But perhaps you should prefer, whenever and wherever it is that you have actually read thus far, to put this book aside now, and either write your own conclusion or take some other option.

conclusions : changing viewpoints

The world has moved on. Yeats's lifetime saw a considerable development across a wide range of technologies of communication and transport, but the decades since his death have seen an even more astonishing expansion and rapidation of new technologies. These have resulted not just in a further shrinking of the globe, but in a displace-ment of the very notion of the world as a place, in at least two aspects, those concerning space and cyber-space.

Some crucial images now resonate differently for us. Yeats spoke of the wide windows of Lissadell opening onto the view: that characteristic country-house out-look. Raymond Williams long ago alerted us to the structure of feeling embodied in that familiar attitude, in so much bourgeois drama, of turning towards a window, looking out upon a world beyond, either in a mood of frustrated waiting, as in Chekhov's *Three Sisters*, or in anxious expectation of some news of crisis. So, often, we wait by the window, in spectatorial mode. A slightly later sensibility focused on that particular form of window watching, the railway carriage window: think of how many film scenes centre on those glances through the reflected countryside, as it speeds past. Or that other consumerist mode, dating back at least to Walter Benjamin's arcades, of window shopping: the society of the spectacle lit up in Regent Street or Oxford Street.

Now the structure of feeling has shifted again, and the dominant overtone of the term 'window' is arguably its reference to a form of graphical user interface, to describe a way of visually organising the representation of data on a computer screen. The Windows operating system and user-interface brings together notions of information and of transport, of navigating through a certain kind of space within the computer, a window giving us access onto that space, but a data space rather than a physical location. Increasingly, the notion of multiple windows operates as a metaphor for multiple modes of being in the world, so that 'real life' can become just another window on a screen already cluttered with openings onto other electronic presences, communities, and identities. As each individual's computer links into a world-wide network of other computers, the conflation of transport and communication metaphors underpins the term 'information super-highway', or the phrase adopted by Bill Gates as the title of his 1995 book *The Road Ahead.* Noticeably, the road figured on the cover of Gates's book seems to be a collage, a digital composite rather than any specific location, an image of distance and direction, without any actual presence.

The image of the house, too, figures largely in Gates's visions of that road ahead. Gates has taken several years to plan and build his own dream house, his experiment in the kind of domestic technologies we might all one day come to accept, and buy. His ideal house is to act as itself a kind of node on the information super-highway. When a visitor enters the Gates house, he or she is tagged electronically, with a link to information about that visitor's tastes and preferences, accessed by the house's built-in database. Not only will the visitor's route through the house be tracked by the observant computer, with light levels, access to rooms, and phone call re-routings adjusted accordingly, but throughout the visitor can be accompanied by their personalised music, wafting with them from room to room, the volume adjustable at a mere whisper of command.

But additionally the walls, or some of them, will be neither ordinary walls nor ordinary windows, but electronic windows onto the wondrous world of a digital image database. Just as the visitor's preferences in music and sound will be accommodated, so their visual pleasure will be catered for by having the walls dissolve into large-scale digital reproductions of their favourite pictures. (Gates is buying the digital rights to 'the million most interesting images' in the world). There is something both appealing and unconsciously crass about this notion. Ruskin evinced a quite alternative attitude when he insisted that all the Turner paintings in his house should be veiled from view, the covering curtains drawn aside only when someone specifically wished to look at a particular painting.

Electronic image-walls are indicative of several wider shifts. In eighteenth century polite society, it was the practice to have on one's walls pictures of rooms in other houses, where one had once lived. (A series of such paintings is usefully reproduced in Mario Praz's *History of Interior Decoration.*) Having paintings or other images reproduced will allow one to reconstruct an apparent environment, rather like the shifting room-scenes at the end of the film *2001,* or those blue-room studios which allow virtual 'sets' to be changed at the press of a button. The environment in which we live becomes as malleable as the identities we might choose to assume in a role-playing game on the Internet.

What this implies is drawn out by those avid players or on-line participants in electronic or virtual communities who recognise that part of the attraction of the net as a way of life is the capacity to build one's own fantasised house in electronic form. [*The draft reads:* Insert quote from Turkle. *I can no longer idenitfy this intended quotation.*] The attractive Situationist slogan, that everyone should live in their own cathedral, can now be given a form of realisation in the power to construct a kind of personalised palace, in the bytes of *Habitat* or its successors. William Mitchell's book *City of Bits* goes further and envisages an entire digital substitute for all those social interactions which have previously been institutionalised in buildings, once familiar as features of our urban landscape: the theatre, bank, library, town hall, newspaper office, and cinema. All these can, in the future, be available in a digital parallel world. There may even be some continuing and constantly updated links to residual 'real-world' data, in the form of David Gelernter's ' mirror worlds'. What happens to any notions of *Gemeinschaft*, or of Raymond Williams's 'known communities' is then unpredictable. In the sim-cities of the future perhaps quite new forms of social relationship will emerge—as with the on-line 'friends' who have never actually met 'in real life'.

home pages

The image of a 'home page' on the world wide web or internet now conflates location, address and identity, a collage or composite of interests, causes and issues, which the individual owner or composer of the home page wishes publicly to be associated with, including chosen links to other home pages on the web. A home page can be given a three-dimensional appearance and may even be designed to look like my actual sitting room, office or garden. (I can represent myself as permanently sitting in my garden, reading Yeats, if I so wish.) But how that home page looks may instead bear no relation to my actual physical surroundings. A composite non-space, a fictive world, can be constructed even more easily than in those experiments in false location of the early days of film-editing, where an actor shot in St. Petersburg would be edited into location footage from Berlin or London or New York. We can now achieve such film effects digitally, of course. But so can any web-site designer with access to an image bank or a scanner. I can composite my home page from a picture of the drawing room of the Frick Museum (image copyright permitting), or of the Taj Mahal, or of Santa's north pole.

Some anticipations of this manufacture of virtual or fictive space have been familiar for some time in the audio realm, in the projection of fantastic living spaces in radio drama, or the capacity of some plausible telephone callers to convince you that you are talking to an opulent businessman in an impressive downtown skyscraper, when the actual shell company may be no more than a phone in a bed-sit. Fortunes have been made in that mode, and no doubt will be again in new digital scams.

But such modes don't just affect our sense of the specific space in which an interlocutor is located. They also change the very concept of space, as the assured framework for overall interactions. Again, radio has given us some anticipations. In Ernst Toller's 1927 play, *Hoppla, We're Alive!*, throughout the scene-changes an actor in an attic at the top of the hotel set was visible twiddling the dials on a radio and picking up live whatever global broadcasts were audible as the play was performed, in real time. A palpable image of a global world already traversed by invisible nets of information, with random access, unpredictable encounters built into that operation, distances and time-zones audibly liberated from spatial constraints. For a whole generation, the experience of listening to war-time broadcasts constituted a form of both family and national community, both formation and definition. Subsequently, a 1950s BBC radio programme, *Forces Favourites*, was devoted to bringing music to the far-flung soldiers of a dwindling empire. The format of the programme consisted of a presenter in London successively linking up with announcers in Cyprus, Aden, India, Australia, or wherever the British crown still saw fit to station troops, and relaying requests for pieces of music both ways, to and from families at home in England and sons (it was mainly sons) serving overseas. On one memorable occasion, the London end of the global inter-links went inexplicably dead for several minutes, and suddenly those subordinate overseas presenters were faced with having to communicate directly with each other, without the centralising interventions and organising supervision of the London announcer. It was a moment in which the relations of a post-colonial world were audibly and emblematically displayed for several moments.

The digital electronic equivalent today is that sense of the world wide web as having no effective centre, though the equivalent to the BBC, in terms of controlling access and manipulating content, may quickly prove to be the profit-driven commercial providers of internet services. The battle being waged over control of the net is indicative of the straining of relations between technical potential and received financial priorities and forms of organisation.

But if, under whatever financial arrangements, information increasingly becomes globally accessible and available, then the status and function of educational institutions may rapidly wither. We could well be faced with the home as quite genuinely the centre of university-level education, as the access point, without ever leaving it, for the best available, as well as the worst in entertainment or voyeurism These are themes for treatment elsewhere, though they indicate one direction for further development of the function of the 'house' as the centre, possibly or optimistically, of 'laughing eagle thoughts that grow'.

cosmic house

The other major change in our perception of the world since the death of Yeats in 1939 has been through the impact of space flight, most obviously in those memorable images of earth as seen from orbit, from moon flights, from the moon itself, and from longer range probes *en route* to Mars or the outer planets. To see the curvature of the world in a port-hole, to see the earth rising above the lunar horizon, to see the blue swirl of the planet isolated against the black backdrop of deep space, was to experience, for the first generation to see it, an extraordinary shift of perspective. Even for those familiar with such images from birth, the implications have been profound. Much of that early impact was due to the combined effect of space-travel and television: it was the television images which initially stunned a global population, though the photographic still images have perhaps endured in their impact far more, as that grainy black-and-white and grey lunar television footage looks increasingly like outmoded early film.

What emerged from that phase was the notion of 'the home planet', a phrase used as the title of a book by a collective of world astronauts published in 1988. From the perspective of space, it became obvious that nobody on earth had a 'special' position *vis à vis* any other. National boundaries were invisible from space. Any map-based image of the world, as divided into coloured segments and crossed with grid-lines of longitude and latitude, became displaced by that overwhelming sense of the physical contours of the earth, the massiveness of that sheer physical terrain compared with any human traces upon it. At the same time, the fragility of human presence was registered in another dimension: that of the alarmingly narrow atmospheric band—to see the thin curtain of breathable air barely visible on the earth's rim was to be made aware of just how vulnerable human presence is, how we share a limited resource of quite terrifying scarcity.

The combined impact of a view-point from space and computer-generated information-processing has perhaps been even more far-reaching than the original influence of global radio and television communications. Satellite surveillance initially seemed mainly of military value, tracking hostile missile sites or troop movements. But once weather satellites began to influence our ways of thinking about meteorology, something far more radical was implicit. It was not simply that previous weather predictions had been mainly parochial, that weather was seen as a matter of local climate, each country having somehow a climate attached to it, with presumed implications for such notions as national character or even personality traits. Some of this had even seemed plausible. But once it was possible to see for ourselves, on a real-time basis, the global patterns of weather formation, the scale of climactic organisation, the genuine connections between an air turbulence over Mexico and a tropical storm developing from it, showering great quantities of rain on Japan several hours later, then it was no longer possible to think of the earth as primarily a matter of nation-states. These were so manifestly subordinate to forces larger and less controllable than national electorates. Global warming was only the most dramatic and worrying insight derived from this shift of perspective.

Something of the same awareness became inescapable with the development of other newly accessible global patternings: visualisations of global movements in other spheres, especially the financial. Though some atlases had attempted to display, through various forms of layerings and mappings, different and converging kinds of information—global patterns of power and communication, of financial flows, arms-sales, nutrition patterns, global resources, energy consumption—these attempts tended to be difficult to update, or to demonstrate convincingly and easily the dynamic aspects of such differential allocations. What global information-processing permitted was a genuine sense of the flows of power and the weather-like patterns of financial movements, the comparability between weather formations and the crises of stock exchanges and inflation processes. A drastic re-modelling of the global economy became possible with the new maths appropriate to these phenomena, though the main benficiaries, and exploiters, of this new possibility were financial institutions themselves.

Though certain foci became the sources for much of this information and for received ways of organising it for presentation, especially on television, mainly in terms of a narrow concentration on the London, Tokyo and New York stock exchanges, what also became apparent was that, again, there was no fixed centre to this swirling of activities. A trading floor in Pittsburgh could momentarily be as globally influential as one in Hong Kong, and both could have major effects beyond anything anticipated or planned in London. An investment decision in the Philippines or Israel could effectively be a global decision in its implications, not geographically confined in any meaningful sense even though national laws might endeavour to intervene. A constantly turning globe has no centre.

cosmic special / ordinary

A further shift of viewpoint was also implicit in the combined impact of space, television, and computer information. Though it was possible to react to that image of a tiny earth isolated against the deep blackness of space with a terrifying sense of the vulnerability, insignificance, or sheer sense of the oddity of the whole globe, set against that backcloth, it was also possible to react with peculiar emotional ambivalence. As it became increasingly possible to visualise the immensity of space and to perform the necessary calculations of its cosmic composition, to recognise the scale of the universe beyond our immediate reach, it also became peculiarly uncertain just how extra-ordinary or otherwise this planet was and is.

The immediate impression of the earth seen against the starry darkness of the rest of this solar system is that it is indeed unique. No evidence of ongoing life elsewhere in the solar system has emerged from all the probes and analyses so far conducted, and this now seems unlikely to be overturned. As far as this solar system is concerned, this globe of rock and water and air is the only current carrier of any life-form. Seen from space, earth is quite simply the only home we have, and it can strike us, perhaps for that reason, as a peculiarly beautiful home to have: there is at some level a reaction of appreciation for those blue and white patterns, though this is for most of us an effect of good photography and selective colour enhancement. The same aesthetic reaction can be registered in relation to other parts of the cosmos: the striking clusters of star formation processes or the disintegrations of enormously massive supernova.

Within this relatively local perspective, this is indeed a special planet. But the argument has been that this earth surely cannot be the only planet with life in the entire universe. The argument comes down to two contrasting calculations. One is based on the immeasurable size of the universe, the billions of stars, and presumably the planet systems around at least some of those stars, and therefore the sense that statistically there must indeed be life elsewhere if there is life here. Against this, is the equally powerful assertion that the odds against any life being on earth at all are so astronomically high that the comparable odds against such an unbelievable coincidence of factors being repeated anywhere else are simply too high for even the number of possibilities indicated by the size of the universe: it simply isn't extensive enough to allow the possibility of a repeat performance against those statistical odds. It then becomes an even more poignant issue as to whether this, our own home planet, might one day—to adopt Yeats's phrase—become 'too ruinous', or stupidly ruined, to support the only life forms we know to exist.

cosmic moral luck

A peculiar repeat of a now familiar pattern emerges at this point. One word we might well use to describe this extraordinary sequences of chances is 'luck'. We, as the human race, are statistically lucky to be alive at all. The only other kind of appropriate word might be some variation of 'owe' rather than 'own': we might believe we owe it to some other process than luck, a creator or a divinity, or perhaps some cosmic force that has made us, with a fiendish sense of finesse and timing, by the skin of our teeth. Thus, old theological arguments loom.

If we assume that for all practial purposes we are indeed the only special planet in the cosmos, a unique house for human life, this also has implications for every life-form on the planet. Each human individual on this planet is unique in a literal sense: each is a unique combination not only of genes, so that genetic fingerprinting is possible, but also each human brain's composition and configuration is unique. Each human brain has a neural connection count of something like 100 billion, and there are as many neurons in my skull as there are stars in the entire known universe. No-one else can possibly have exactly the same set of neural net connections as myself, the same convoluted and changing patterns of synaptic connections, organically grown and constantly modified by ongoing feed-back processes. Moreover, each one of us is also unique because each body has its own continuing relation to such mundane parameters as physical location and temporal allocation—whatever the range of digital subsitutes that might some day become available to us in a virtual mode. I can only exist in one time-space and nobody else can occupy that same segment of the spatio-temporal matrix—which means that each of us has to have a unique history.

Yet all this seems to have made very little difference to how we treat these unique specimens. The history of 'moral atrocity' from the Irish famine to Biafra or Bosnia is an utterly chilling reminder of how such irreplaceable entities can be dismissed into oblivion. Children are the species's way of continuing uniqueness. Any killing of a child is therefore a closure of a whole line of possible human development. We recognise that fact in animal species, that the very last tiger will leave a hole in the species layer which can never be replaced, despite attempts to revive dinosaurs from dormant DNA. Equally, the pre-mature death of a single human being can leave a gap in the transmission chain which can never be replaced. But that chain is not of course predictable: the inter-play of choice and chance in mating partners leaves it an open question. Children remain, however, the greatest moral luck gamble we take.

And now the planet itself is also, it seems, subject to considerations of moral luck, if we take a further shift of view-point and see this planet not just from our own perspective but from that of the universe as a whole. If it is indeed the case that life is so scarce that we and all the other life-forms on this planet may even be its only exemplar, then a dizzying perspective opens up, rather similar to that opened up on earth a few centuries ago when people first thought they could one day fly, or when people first thought there might even be a world beyond the visible horizon.

In the post-war period, with historically astonishing speed, the notion of space travel within our local solar system has been given practical realisation, albeit fraught with difficulties and real dangers for some. In the 1990s what was emerging was a realistic commitment to space exploration and settlement. And not just within the solar system, though escaping from the solar system may today seem as difficult to envisage as escaping earth gravity must have seemed a few centuries ago.

If space settlement is to be possible then the presence of life on this planet, and perhaps uniquely so, becomes an extraordinary aspect of our status in the universe. There is a massive moral luck question hovering over us all. If 'our' luck is to travel to and eventually settle on, and possibly terra-form, a multitude of other planets, not just in this tiny solar system but beyond—which is now a perhaps feasible proposition, though as fraught with difficulties as getting to the moon seemed one hundred years ago—then Yeats's question in 'Upon a House' begins to suggest another variation on its lines which is not merely rhetorical:

> How should the universe be luckier if this world,
> . . . . became too ruinous
> To breed the human eyes that love the sun?

This home planet may indeed carry a strange kind of 'responsibility', in which no individual on it is to be seen as either 'special' or simply 'ordinary', since the scale of comparison (the universe itself . .) makes that distinction im-measurable. We are all peculiarly privileged, as a tiny blip of life which is possibly due to grow beyond our planet. When only a handful of apes managed to talk, any one of them would have been a planetary loss. In the wide-spread versions of the 'Noah' story, it was recognised as essential to keep at least one representative of each species safe from the flood. The 'Cain and Abel' story may be read as lamenting that a whole line of descent, indeed half the latent possibilities of human life, may have been wiped out almost from the 'beginning'. We all, it has to be recognised, owe our existence to the mere fact that someone, somewhere, did not kill our common ancestor. The latest estimate is that only five extended families populated the whole of Europe.

Of course, we do not have a merely passive relation to that possible species future. And to its immense cost. It might seem that other demands are more pressing. That the currently starving millions across the globe have no interest in, no possible investment or stake in, how a tiny percentage of the globe chooses to devote itself to the immensely long-range possibilities of space travel. True. And the gamble is a gamble. There is now a distinct danger that this planet may itself become—or be deliberately and stupidly rendered—'too ruinous' to breed more life, a few decades or perhaps a few centuries hence. Without the expansion possibilities of a wholly new frontier, the planet may reach the saturation point of its resources. In any case, it will perhaps only avoid doing so at the expense of other species which we may one day realise, retrospectively and regretfully, that we needed for environments and scenarios we cannot yet conceive.

Yet on what basis do we make these comparisons and decisions? Measured against what? Do we compare the billions on this planet with the potential zillions of a populated universe? Or compare the time perspectives of the next explosive population generation as against either the last 100 years (when Yeats was writing) or the next thousand, or a million, years of the future?

Kim Stanley Robinson's *Mars* trilogy and the UN's recent Millenium Project offer their possible or at least plausible notions of a global future. There are, of course, others. Popular film has provided a variety of scenarios over the past decades, many of them pessimistic or dystopic, from AI machines taking over the world to disease-ridden mutants slowly exterminating the last remaining viable humans. Extra-terrestrial conquests of the earth seem currently rather out of fashion, though some believers are still waiting for the landing of those who will redeem us, or enslave us. Pan-galactic star wars as projections of our parochial wars on earth seem still to have considerable box office appeal, though it may be the sense of immense technical progress in their special effects that appeals as much as the casually murderous firepower wielded.

More sober-minded and fact-based extrapolations tend to focus on artificial intelligence and artificial life scenarios, with eventual evolutionary displacement of humans as the carriers of further cosmic development, including the possibility of launching artificial intelligence and artificial life forms onto far-flung space-travel ahead of any possible human explorations. Or nano-technology may be offered as a way of resolving, for some time at least, the problems of resourcing the needs of a growing global population, coupled with extrapolations of tchnically possible control mechanisms over artificially distorted wealth distribution, and even over natural forces—all of which promises or hopes arguably become progressively less plausible as they approach the ambition of total control. The forces not made by human-kind seem at some level always to recede beyond our increasing control—dreams of nuclear fusion energy or an anti-gravity device still beckon. . . Other technologies can attract distinct sectoral interests and investment, such as a future society spent in a fully virtual environment. In much science fiction several combinations of these technical possibilities are combined with others not yet imaginable in sufficient detail to be scientifically assessable. In some actual projects, such as the Argos Venture initiated by Michael Young, the task of constructing and operating a practical mock-up on earth of a feasible Mars living environment has brought together these several possible technologies, as well as raising intriguing issues concerning the possible cultural forms such a project might involve and evolve.

But in all such scenarios and extrapolations, predictions and anticipations, there remains perhaps a rather curious sense of gap, a hole in the fabric of postulation. The future, it can seem, has already been so extensively imagined in the recent past, during that epoch of cold war paranoia, hostility, and projection, that it is difficult to invent a genuinely new set of operative values with any plausibility, even any urgently sane and sensible green scenarios. It has become difficult to imagine any desirable future in the abstract, as for example in those few films which broke the mould of red-baiting parable: such imagined close encounters could offer little more in the way of a desirable future than rather elegantly thin aliens and a great deal of bright light and SFX vastness. Quite what one might be travelling to the stars in order to experience or to implant was left remarkably vague. Necessarily so perhaps. For unless we have a terrestrial set of goals that are worth realising, it is impossible to imagine a civilisation which has realised them, except in the very vaguest terms: the peace, security, and happiness still redolent of ideological justifications for their opposite..

cosmic gnomon

The need for shared global goals is apparent in their very absence. It was an odd consequence of that cold war epoch that the world did become globalised, did indeed become seen as a single system. The so-called world wars of the first half of the 20th century never really became global occasions in the sense implied by the term. Not simply because some countries remained ostensibly neutral, or some on-going processes escaped being sucked into the conflict. The extraordinary Satyajit Ray film *The Chess Players* presents the always appealing possibility of continuing to play games while war and disaster gathers. But in the post-1945 period it could be claimed that everything on earth became politicised into that opposition of just two camps. Had Ethiopia not been part of that perception, seen as a suspect ally of the Soviets, would 'Western ' aid have been so slow in reaching it? Any local conflict could be, and normally was, linked into that two-way split. It was impossible to initiate a minor land reform in Peru without the powerful forces of an American boycott being deployed. It was impossible for Afghanistan peasants to take up arms against a Soviet-backed government without covert control by the CIA. And so on, everywhere and always, for decades.

One effect of that fully global conflict was precisely the development of those technologies now being given their commercial and partly non-military application. It is highly doubtful if any of the investment in space-travel, communication satellites, information processing, or even in the development of personal computers and the internet would have occurred for primarily commercial reasons, still less for purely scientific reasons. (So much for claims of capitalists investing in radical innovation?). The drive was military and the ambition was to seize an advantage over an enemy. Now that ever-threatening ideological opponent is (temporarily) consigned to the ash-can of history, the question emerges of what is to take its place. One scenario has Islam promptly sliding into the vacated seat as a global ideological enemy, justifying a further round of military expenditure and political paranoia.. One awkward problem is that Islamic power also controls much of global oil. So we can expect Gulf war scenarios as well as the usual support of oil-rich sheiks against their own populations. Familiar scenarios. But perhaps less 'satisfactory' than before, since in the currently dominant uni-polar ideology there is again perpetuated an unrealisable image (literally, in the case of global advertising seductions) of a certain always-fulfillable but-not-yet future of affluence and unlimitedl consumption, which is bound to lead to the re-emergence of sporadic liberation movements and occasional revolutionary struggles, however ideologically perceived by their protagonists. A predictable cycle begins again. Includuing, no doubt, alleged rough beasts slouching towards Jerusalem.

The effect of the 1945-89 global conflict was a form of negative unification, a unity in contrary as the logicians might say. After 1989, we saw an odd kind of victory without a defeat, since the 'American side' could not plausibly (though they did) claim credit for several populist revolts and for the internal collapse of the Soviet regime. This left 'American' hegemony apparently unchallenged, yet without any universal acceptance, as might have followed from a successfully imposed or, even more, a genuine victory over hearts and minds. For much of the globe, 'America ' remains the enemy, but not in terms of some alignment with nostalgia for a defeated and bankrupt Soviet model. That too had often been an enemy. But American national or state power is now a residue, awaiting its own demise, though presumably not in terms of any revived appeal to Soviet forms and policies as a properly viable alternative. Nor perhaps is this coming cycle to be characterised primarily by the emegence to dominance of some new 'great power', the nation-states of Japan or China, India or Brazil, though that may still be the media-plausible form that now more crucial modes of domination continue to take, which are not primarily national in character at all, 'American' or otherwise. The crucial shape that global conflict may increasingly take, at the visible as well as the structural levels, may be that between global institutions and more or less dis-associated individuals, unified dominance versus impotent fragmentation: the relation between a trans-national bank and its customer(s) is decidedly not that between an industrial corporation and its unionised work-force.

As regards available dominant or influential discourses, compelling descriptions, or plausible explanations, various alternative or perhaps complementary ways of perceiving our emergent futures can be preferred or chosen: for example, those focused upon gender or ecology, racial justice or religious allegiance. Yet throughout these contending voices, there seems to be a persistent double awareness: that there is both a need for and an absence of any shared global value system, a set of convergent goals, a framework of accepted evaluation. Even the hard-won legal provisions against 'crimes against humanity', an after-effect of the (almost) undeniable world war atrocities, can be evaded, denied, or blatantly repudiated, when it is a matter of war crimes by one's own people, military personnel, or political allies.

One way of putting this is that we now have an ideology-shaped hole in our political consciousness, a hole which by its very absence defines the overall incomplete shape from which it has been excised. I have discussed this elsewhere, in relation to James Joyce's use of the geometry term 'gnomon' in *Dubliners*, but we can register it most palpably in the patent hollowness of our prevailing political discourse, where there seems little of either 'passion' or 'precision', still less an honest fusion of both.

We simply can no longer speak that familiar politicians' language with any credibility or conviction, as Joyce's young boy could not mouth the official language of religious mourning when faced with an actual death—yet we have no other. To speak the discourse of professional politicians is to satirise it, but in the light of what criteria are we judging it to be deficient? It is the best we have, and it is not good enough, but we do not know what would be good enough. An occasional rhetorical resonance might briefly interrupt the bland formulaic flows, that of a Mandela perhaps, but the shallowness of our political forms are perhaps most visible in the absence, in this image-saturated and media-shaped world, of any compelling ritualization, still less widely endorsed celebration, of the necessary political processes, debate, and negotiation. The echoes come:

How but in custom and in ceremony
Are innocence and beauty born?

On the television news, we see a group of men (overwhelmingly, men) in ordinary business suits walking down some kind of corridor, nondescript, into a familiar banal setting, desks and chairs laid out in a circle or ellipse. It could be the meeting of a county cricket club or of a small company, a parish council or a university sub-committee. Or it could be crucial and urgent peace talks between Israel and Palestine. Or an emergency session of a United Nations crisis team faced with another and more disastrous Chernobyl.

From one perspective, this is even encouraging: showing us that at least the forms of power have a certain accessible similarity across the various levels and stages of power, a degree of democratic appearance, an ordinariness. At another, however, it seems to provide visual confirmation for what we already widely acknowledge: that 'the gifts that govern men' are increasingly, at best, only those of a continual talking performance, without effective purchase upon the processes of impersonal corporate power and morally indifferent decision that so determinedly shape our world: that, indeed, 'the gifts that govern men' no longer govern.

back to Yeats

If we are to understand Yeats's poems in their relation to the complex history I have been sketching, in however a simplified way, do we therefore need first to attempt the awkward task of understanding that very term 'history' itself?

There is, of course, an initial problem in thinking of 'history' or 'histories'. There are at least three main senses of the term. The clearest distinction, to begin with, is that between history as meaning what is written and history as meaning what has happened. That distinction itself becomes, of course, immediately complicated. Some would maintain that the only history we have is that which has been 'written', in some form, that history is a matter of the records, that only through those records do we know or think we know 'what happened': we have no other access. Indeed, there is nothing other to which we might have access: the past exists only in and as the various material traces left in the present; history simply is those 'texts'.

Others would say that whatever is written as 'history'can never comprehend 'what happened' because the writing (in all its forms, from original 'source' to completed treatise) can only be, at best, a kind of map and the map can never be co-terminous with the terrain. What happened will always exceed our attempts to say what happened, even at the time.

But there is then a further distinction lurking, between two senses of 'what happened'. If history is what happened, then it includes what happened yesterday as I tripped over a stone on the pavement and stubbed my toe, or what happened this morning as I re-read Yeats in my garden, as well as whatever 'happened' in Petrograd in 1917 or 'what happened', say, in India from the 4th to the 8th century, however one calibrates those times. It is the relation between those two senses that constitutes part of the writing problem, not only because my casual diarybriefly recording a sunny afternoon or a painful toe can, if it survives, become part of the written traces, available for the record alongside all other survivals—Yeats's poems, Lady Gregory's journal, statistics of income and ownership, political manifestos, newspaper reports, recorded broadcasts, the internet archive—to be sifted and selected and interpreted, but leaving the problem of articulating a stubbed toe onto the sweep of continental and epochal changes: the sheer intractibility of any compositional form, 'writing history', that can include Cleopatra's nose and the fall of an empire, a king's vanity and demographic trends, a ruined house and outer space..

Obviously, a myopic restriction to the mundaneities of a journal, the microscopic of a diary, can preclude the possibility of any larger canvas, a Grand Narrative of 'what happened' in the old sense. Yet to appeal to the very notion of a Grand Narrative is to appeal, it can be claimed, to a specifically 'Western' mode of historiography, a claim that there is a perspective from which global history can legitimately be perceived. Sir Walter Raleigh, South American buccaneer and owner of an Irish plantation, was perhaps the first to attempt a 'History of the World', and the notion that the 'world' can have 'a history' is congruent with those other emergent modes of sixteenth-century Europe which characterise, one could claim (within a Grand Narrative), the moment of Western imperial expansion. Ireland's lasting subjugation is then a moment within that moment. Both Foster's *Modern Ireland* and Friel's *Making History* take 1600 as their pivot date.

To combat the very notion of the 'Grand Narrative' might then be seen, as in much 'post-colonial' writing and new historiography, as the refusal to endorse the West's view of its own expansion. Though it is clear that quite often even the attempt to avoid or sidestep the claims of Grand Narrative, of global imperialist history, is itself implicitly placed against certain crucial moments within that Grand Narrative. There remain, it would seem, 'world-historical events', though which they are is always a matter for retrospective affirmation. One might have said, in 1917, 1918, or 1919, that the Soviet Revolution in its own terms, in the terms in which its agents would themselves explain it, was indeed a world historical event: here the working class was taking control of its own destiny for the first time in human history—this was the end of pre-history. Such terms might be plausible or otherwise; but they are different from an appeal to a quite other criterion, which is whether, nearly a century on, it is the case that, wherever on the globe one might go, the ordinary condition of life is still shaped by the fact of the Soviet Revolution and its long aftermath. By contrast, the Dublin Easter rising of 1916 was not a world-historical event — though it might possibly have turned out to be so, given a different outcome and different events elsewhere. If, for example, the 1917 Soviet rising under Lenin had immediately failed while Ireland had achieved a socialist-inclined liberation from British colonial power, under the leadership of James Collins, a quite different world history would then have resulted. It didn't.

One problem with any such 'retrospective' perspective is that though it leaves open which events are eventually to be regarded as world-historical events, and by whom, any such notion does tend to leave any contribution of one's own—that other level of 'what happened', to me, yesterday, the stubbed toe, reading a book, or even the birth of my daughter—as endemically marginal and wholly unimportant within the perspective of world history. This is not, of course, to exclude the point that what is presented as a world-historical confrontation between, say, the USA and the USSR, or Capitalism and Communism, might itself be seen as relatively marginal to some other global perspective, in which the struggle is seen as between, say, Islam and Christianity, or poor and rich, or east and west, north and south, or even Microsoft versus Apple, Barclays versus HSBC. All these terms offer competing perspectives, and I would have to claim that my assessment of any articulation between them rests upon my own consideration of which provides the more enclosing explanation, the fuller and more adequately comprehensible intelligibility of the global situation—insofar as I, or anyone, can grasp it.

Yet I, too, occupy some definite place, however marginal or provincial, within that 'history ' which is to be made intelligible, and the remaining difficulty is to think through that relation. We are back to the problem of thinking the very concept of history. Let me use a kind of analogy, drawn from basic mathematics.

Faced by a complicated mathematical equation, and trying to 'solve' it, I might be completely stuck, unable even to make sense of the problem as formulated, even to see why it constitutes itself as an equation—until someone points out that the equation deploys the concept of square root, which to me is a new concept. I might then find myself both beginning to understand the concept of square root and resolve the given equation into intelligibility simultaneously, as—equipped with some understanding of what this new concept might mean—I begin to follow through what it might do in practice, in the actual composition of this particular equation. It seems to me that, for example, Marx's concepts such as 'surplus value' or 'alienation' offer themselves as concepts of a similar kind, in this respect, to that of 'square root'. We need, as it were, the concept of surplus value to understand the historical struggle for the eight-hour day, but it is only by engaging in, or following through, that struggle in its details, that one fully understands, by a kind of reciprocal feed-back, the concept of surplus value itself, grasps its reach and the depth of its operation, its intricate centrality to the whole economic structure within which a fight for reduced working time takes place: the formally equal but un-equal equation at the core of the wage-relation which is worked out in all its ramified effects, those effects being the concept of 'surplus vlaue', or indeed of 'working time', actually in operation.

One might want to claim that such notions as sexism or racism are also similar in kind. It is only in the struggle to change one's own behaviour, or that of others, in a non-sexist way or non-racist response, that one begins to grasp the full dimensions of what we call sexism or racism. However, with sexism, as with racism, I would tend to say that in the end, whereas surplus value offers an explanatory concept, the notion of racism or sexism only points to what needs to be explained: racism is not itself an explanation for racism, and my growth in understanding of what the term implies and covers is an elaboration, not a resolution, of the equation, an elaboration of what has to be conceptualised and combatted. In that respect, racism and sexism are perhaps more akin to 'capitalism' (which is what needs to be explained) than to 'surplus value'.

The term 'history' seems to be in a third category, though often used as if it were either itself explanatory (history is to blame, it seems, wrote Joyce) or in some sense what has to be explained. Yet it is not so much that history is a concept which might enable me to understand, as it were, the equation; or that history is a shorthand descriptive term for the whole equation. The notion of 'history', I want to suggest, is equivalent in function to the very equation sign in a mathematical equation: the equals sign (=) which makes it an equation. To 'understand' an equals sign is to understand that there is an equation. Any attempt to modify the equation so that it 'balances' in some other and changed way would then be what it would mean to understand the concept ''equals'. When Marx, for example, speaks of political movements or of technological developments as 'changing' history, he points to a process or a task that in one sense we cannot refuse—the equation of actuality always balances whether we like it or not, whether we undertand it or not, whether we consciously try to intervene or not—and our very existence constitutes a component within the ongoing overall ever-actual equation. But it is only by trying in some more deliberate and conscious way to change that equation, to make it balance in some alternative result, that we can begin to understand the depth, complexity, and perplexity, of what we mean by history. .

a final note, or interruption . . .

9th May 2015.

In 1998 I simply left it there. This morning, it became clear that the British Conservatives have gained an unexpected and wholly unpredicted overall majority in the UK General Election. Only about 24% of the eligible electorate voted for a Conservative candidate. Yet this may now mean a referendum on UK membership of the EU, possibly (if only as a result of a vote for EU exit) the independence of Scotland and the break-up of the United Kingdom, a further futile move of the Labour Party towards the bankrupt neo-liberal economic consensus, and future victories for the Tories anyway in a rump UK, consisting of England and a few Welsh and Northern Ireland constituencies—but perhaps thereby re-opening the issue also of the re-unification of an Ireland still within the EU…

So why publish this short book on Yeats, now? In part, simply because the recent shifts in publishing and printing technologies mean that I can now do so without necessarily wasting trees or any publisher's investment in it—only copies actually ordered need be printed, and I can in any case offer digital download versions of any books I now publish (if the various e-pub formats can solve the problem of preserving decent page lay-out and, importantly, proper foot-notes). And therefore why not? All it takes is my time. And, if you choose to read it, your time. There is already too much to be read, and too much not worth reading. And now not only personal home pages or websites, but blogs, tweets, Facebook entries, YouTube channels, and so on. In that context, I think, without being sure, that this book too is—for some people at least—as worth reading as much that is already available. Though any readers will probably have to find this book by chance. And I recognise, of course, that all publishing involves—as Yeats well knew—both arrogance and self-indulgence.

I recall the interesting and well-intentioned advice given me when I first graduated: "Don't publish a book before you're 40." I first drafted this book when I was forty. I am now seventy, and see it perhaps differently. I have in the meanwhile written other books or parts of books, several of which I never bothered to try to publish. I might not have found a sympathetic publisher for them anyway, of course, but in any case there always seemed more pressing things to do.

For wholly personal reasons, there aren't too many more pressing things I can do now. Arthritis has reduced me to merely sitting at a laptop most of the day, and dictating rather than scribbling by hand. I can of course sign petitions and contribute to the various feedback and comment sites. Since I can still, after a fashion, also write, or at least copy-edit, I do so. Motivation enough perhaps. And, as a related further consideration, like any retired academic, I would rather like to spare my children the hassle of wondering whether to decide which, if any, of the many tattered typescripts and dusty print-outs which litter my study, and which of the files and folders which clutter my computers, might possibly be worth salvaging. So I will publish, shortly, as much as I want to dredge for the moment, and the rest of the bulging box-files and piles of paper can cheerfully be burned.

Nevertheless, these purely personal motives don't, of course, justify my taking up your time. If you have read thus far, you will no doubt have already decided that issue for yourself. But let me briefly add some further relevant considerations.

This long and deliberately segmented essay has been partly concerned with the sometimes suppressed or undeclared relations between a personal response or situation and the professional practices and conventions of 'literary criticism', and perhaps of academic discourses in general. In part, the essay has been an experiment in mildly modifying those relations. One specific factor prompting my response, it has to be said, is that I came from what Mr Yeats would undoubtedly have described as 'mean roof trees' —though I have, in his terms, been strangely lucky.

The essay has also been concerned with exploring or unfolding the relations between a 'local habitation' and a global frame: indeed, between any local habitation, including my own, and implicitly yours, and whatever is the current global equation. I happen, by now, to live in, and indeed to co-own, a house which in the circumstances of my time and place can hardly operate as either the Coole Park of Yeats's poem or as the Surrey House with which I compared it—though the ludicrous state of the UK housing market since Thatcher means that I should perhaps now re-write the segment on Lady Gregory's £800. Certainly, the poem has taken on further resonances since I first tried to write about it.

In particular, it is now clearly the case that we no longer need to trace elaborate chains of connection between a specific house and a global crisis. Every time I switch on the central heating, or even a light bulb or a kettle, my relation to the looming ruination of the plant is undeniable. And, equally clearly, the imperative need, at this historical moment, is for the rapid development and implementation of alternative energy technologies.

Yet, again this very day, the US government of President Obama has announced provisional 'permission' (on whose behalf?) for oil drilling in the Arctic. Currently, over 50% — 131 members — of the Republican caucus in the US House of Representatives deny the occurrence of human-caused global warming, and 70 percent—38 members — on the Senate side take the same position. A recent report released by the CAP Action fund found that, on average, climate change deniers within the Senate received $732,788 from fossil fuel interests in career contributions. On the House side, the 131 climate science deniers have taken $35,702,245 in fossil fuel industry contributions. One recalls Sir William's £3 'gratification' in the Dublin parkliamentary election. The 'gifts that govern men' seems more and more a bitterly ironic phrase.

It remains the case, however, that any house, or home, or educational institution, or even a party headquarters, is still open to the kinds of question which I, through Yeats, have asked in this essay—and the answers, or replies, or responses, might take several forms. For me, one response, for several years, was to "Give up literary criticism!" —as Ludwig Wittgenstein memorably barked at F. R. Leavis. Another, at this moment, is to turn my study and even our whole house, it can sometimes seem, into a small and 'independent' "publishing house"—as they used to be called. Mine is called 'New Crisis Quarterly', for perhaps obvious reasons, and I will now publish several short books in the near future, all inter-linked in some ways—though I expect to find few readers, if any at all, let alone any who will register those inter-connections. My house is not, of course, Coole Park, nor even the Cuala Press, but I will at least use the available technologies to publish my small contributions as cheaply and widely as the publishing process will allow me—since whatever apparent 'independence' I might claim is in practice dependent upon one or more global capitalist companies…

And so the themes of this essay come round again.

This has been one response to the questions of the poem.

Perhaps you should now write and publish your own.

Meanwhile, I will go and read Yeats, again, in my garden.

Segments

reading in time
temporalities
later
reading a poem
relevant historical facts
gifts that govern men
theories of development
Sinn Fein
problems of response
the extra-verbal situation
the Liverpool connection
how should the world
if this house
£800 a year
passion and precision
upon other houses
mere ideology?
moral luck
responsibilities
Easter 1916
choice and chance
reading a poem II
marginal intellectuals
How should the world be luckier . . . .
interruptions
conclusions : changing viewpoints
home pages
cosmic house
cosmic special / ordinary
cosmic moral luck
alt. futures
cosmic gnomon
back to Yeats
a final note

www.ingramcontent.com/pod-product-compliance
Lightning Source LLC
Chambersburg PA
CBHW052356060726
47592CB00020B/2449